IRAN: The Ayatollah's Hidden Hand

Tehran's Covert Campaign to Undermine Its Principal Opposition, the Mujahedin-e Khalq (MEK)

by Ivan Sascha Sheehan, Ph.D.

Copyright © 2023
Iran Policy Committee
Ivan Sascha Sheehan, Ph.D.
1420 N. Charles St.
Baltimore, MD 21201-5779

All rights reserved. No part of this publication may be reproduced or transmitted in any form or by any means, electronic or mechanical, including photocopy, recording or any information storage and retrieval system, without permission in writing from the publisher.

Printed in the United States of America.
First edition.

ISBN (Paperback):   978-1-7342292-3-3
ISBN (e-book):   978-1-7342292-5-7

Library of Congress Control Number:
Library of Congress Cataloging-in-Publication Data

IRAN: The Ayatollah's Hidden Hand
Tehran's Covert Campaign to Undermine Its Principal Opposition, the Mujahedin-e Khalq (MEK)

1. Iran.   2. Khamenei.   3. MEK.   4. Disinformation.   5. Middle East.

First published: November 2023
Printed in the United States of America

Table of Contents

Foreword by Ambassador Lincoln P. Bloomfield, Jr. v

PART I: The Infiltration 1
    Beware of the MEK!. 2
    Iran Experts Initiative (IEI) 4
    Tehran's protectors 6
    U.S. Congress stands firm. 6

PART II: Pro-democracy, anti-regime protests 9
    Waves of social unrest rock the Islamic Republic of Iran 9
    The MEK's threat to a fundamentalist regime 12
    Taking a page from Hitler's playbook 15

Part III: Disinformation and influence operations 19
    Production of movies and TV series defacing the MEK 21
    Publication of books against the MEK 24

Part IV: Security agencies active against the MEK 27
    Owj Arts and Media Organization 27
    The causes of establishing Owj 29
    Financial sources of Owj 29
    What is Owj's mandate? 30
    The decisionmakers 31
    Who is "Esfahani"? 33
    The Ofogh TV Network 35

Part V: From silence to attacks 37
    The MEK's influence. 38
    The threat of overthrow and a "tsunami of fear" 39

Conclusions and policy recommendations 43

Appendix 47
    U.S. Senate Letter to Secretary of Defense 47
    U.S. House of Representatives Letter to Secretary of Defense . . 52

About the author. 55
Iran Policy Committee (IPC) 57
Endnotes 61

Foreword

by Lincoln P. Bloomfield Jr., former Assistant Secretary of State for Political-Military Affairs

TWO FACTORS LARGELY ACCOUNT FOR THE FACT that the US foreign policy community has, for decades now, been serially misinformed about Iran's organized resistance: the Mujahedin-e Khalq (MEK) and its umbrella organization, the National Council of Resistance of Iran (NCRI). A study group formed by student intellectuals in 1965, seeking to liberate Iranian society from the corruption and authoritarian repression of the Shah, the MEK was purely political in nature. Its existence was unknown to the authorities for six years, but they were rounded up by the Shah's security forces in 1971. By 1973, dozens of their members and all but one of the eight leaders had been executed. Yet other, more radical activists adopted the "Mujahedin" name, seeking to capitalize on the prestige of the martyred idealists. They were secular, not Muslim; some had been trained at terror camps in Cuba and East Germany. These were the killers of Americans in Iran during the 1970s.

To the affluent elite of Iran devoted to the Peacock Throne, the domestic unrest of the 1970s was a nightmare, and all student radicals were frightening. The Shah's public relations machine stoked their fears by painting any "Mujahedin" – including the sole surviving MEK leader, Massoud Rajavi, writing books in prison – as dangerous Marxists bent on spilling the blood of their own countrymen. The Shah's demonization of the MEK stuck, carried to the West by upper-class Iranians who fled during the revolution and by many Americans who had worked with them in Iran. It is telling that despite decades of regime terror abroad and tyranny at home, many monarchists now living in the West will more readily denounce the MEK than the clerical dictatorship.

The second factor was also a misunderstood episode and the key to understanding why the ruling clerics have warred non-stop against the MEK for 44 years. After telling his supporters in Paris that he supported democracy and planned to retire to Qom for religious reflection, Ayatollah Khomeini landed in Tehran in February 1979 to a hero's welcome and then unveiled a constitution investing himself as Supreme Leader with the unchallenged authority of the 12th Imam of the Prophet. Asked by Khomeini for his support along with his Muslim intellectual movement – the real MEK – Massoud Rajavi said no, the Iranian people now expected freedom with political rights, not another dictatorship. Thus did the MEK become Khomeini's most feared challenger, questioning the legitimacy of not only his political authority but, far more importantly, his divine religious mandate.

As America obsessed over the hostage crisis, public rallies and leafleting protested the darkening turn to fundamentalism. Khomeini's street militia answered with violence. Iran's first (and only) democratically-elected President stood with Rajavi and was violently impeached. A half-million Iranians filled downtown Tehran on June 20, 1981, with large demonstrations in other cities, answering Rajavi's call to demand their political rights. Khomeini and his clerical lieutenants made the fateful decision to open fire on the crowds, and a reign of terror ensued in which tens of thousands of mostly youthful, educated Iranians were executed, women no less than men. They were called religious "hypocrites," waging "war against God" when, in fact, they died for their belief that Iranians deserve to live in a free country and that Islam can co-exist with political rights and agency.

The mullahs erected a Berlin Wall of secrecy, propaganda, and disinformation at home and abroad, trying in every way to exterminate the MEK and its potent vision of Islam as freedom, undermining Khomeini's "guardianship of the Islamic jurist" (velayat-e faqih). Only years later did the world learn that Khomeini had ordered a massive crime against humanity in which up to 30,000 political prisoners, mostly MEK, were executed in the summer and fall of 1988. Any Iranian expressing support for the MEK risks imprisonment and torture; the law also calls for amputation as a punishment. Should we be surprised that Western visitors to Iran have never heard a positive word uttered about the MEK?

Decades of trying to erase the MEK and its story from domestic and global discourse and foreign governments believing the regime's derogatory narratives have made life very challenging for the organization and its supporters. Yet, the MEK has endured. There is a new generation of MEK activists in the streets of Iran, and they are connected to the NCRI and, even more so, the exiled MEK, which sits in Albania, protected from regime bombers and assassins within a secure campus. Where official media outlets never used to speak of the resistance other than an occasional reference to the "MKO terrorist grouplet," the rising tide of organized protest in Iran has only led the regime to double down on efforts to generate false narratives and propaganda. It is not working.

In this informative and well-presented volume, Professor Ivan Sascha Sheehan pulls back the curtain on the regime's propaganda franchise and reveals the exorbitant investment of funding, infrastructure, and manpower frantically trying to convince Iranians and the world not to believe their own eyes and ears. After years of trying to ignore the MEK, hoping others would do the same, regime officials now seemingly cannot stop talking about how effectively the MEK's message and organizing efforts are empowering the national uprising. Sheehan's research makes clear that the regime is scared, knowing that there really is a blueprint and a competent political organization – run at every level by women – ready to help guide Iran to a legitimate constitutional future when the regime crumbles, just as happened with the Shah.

After absorbing Sheehan's impressive primer on Tehran's formidable "spin" enterprise, readers just might ask themselves how much of what leading Western news organizations, government ministries, NGOs, academics, and Iran-watchers have been telling them for years about the MEK might actually not be true after all.

Professor Sheehan is to be applauded for delivering such a relevant resource. An exposé of this caliber should make a rigorous reexamination of contemporary Iran's history – and policy – as inevitable as it is necessary.

PART I

THE INFILTRATION

A September 2023 revelation by SEMAFOR and Iran International exposed a ring of Iranian-backed influence operatives that had infiltrated the highest ranks of the U.S. government.[1] Having been provided with top-level security clearances, these Iranian agents had access to highly classified and sensitive information available only to senior U.S. officials, placing them in a unique position to mislead American policymakers while undermining policy toward Iran's theocratic regime. The actors allegedly collaborated with and took direction from senior Iranian officials while maintaining the appearance of working on behalf of the U.S. government.

As SEMAFOR noted, at least three of these operatives went straight from soliciting talking points from Tehran to working on Iran policy in the Biden administration under U.S. Special Representative for Iran, Rob Malley – whose security clearance was suspended over questions about his handling of classified information.

While the principal objective of the years long campaign was to influence and derail U.S. policy toward Iran, those involved also prioritized the promotion of a misleading characterization of the leading Iranian opposition group, the Mojahedin-e Khalq or People's Mojahedin Organization of Iran (PMOI/MEK). By seeking to neutralize favorable impressions of the organization among Washington's foreign policy elite, Tehran sought to take down an entity capable of aiding Western attempts to curtail the Iranian regime's nuclear weapons program, malign regional agenda, human rights abuses, and fundamentalist inclinations. By brazenly targeting the highly effective dissident organization, the operatives hoped to leave U.S. officials with the false impression that there is no viable alternative to the ayatollahs – and certainly not one with a pro-democracy record that remains committed to toppling clerical rule.

Beware of the MEK!

In 2014, Ariane Tabatabai, then a predoctoral fellow at Harvard University, published an article that pointedly advised policymakers to "Beware of the MEK."[2] The article leveled strong accusations against the Iranian regime's principal domestic adversary, the MEK, to discourage American and European legislators from backing its pro-democracy commitments.

Tabatabai described the MEK as a "cult-like dissident group based outside of Iran," repeating long-discredited allegations involving acts of terrorism, attacks on Americans, and hostage takings. While noting that the group had been removed from European terrorist lists in 2009 and the U.S. State Department list in 2012, she repeated spurious and long-denied claims that the MEK had attacked American personnel in the 1970s and supported the hostage-taking at the U.S. embassy in Tehran at the end of that decade.

The article accused the MEK of torture, beatings, and controlling "every aspect of its members' lives." While indirectly acknowledging the organization's democratic platform, Tabatabai accused the group of deceiving and manipulating its Western supporters by secretly advancing an ideology that threatened Western security interests. Tabatabai repeated the allegations in widely circulated foreign policy outlets in 2018 and 2020, clearly directing her ire at the ayatollahs' adversary.

Curious analysts at the time might have wondered why a young Iranian-American researcher with a thin publication record would bother to make her maiden publication voyage by attacking the well-known dissident group. Nine years later, it appears that Tabatabai was in close contact with Iranian officials for whom she was effectively serving as a mouthpiece in the United States.

Since then, Tabatabai has rarely missed an opportunity to promote Tehran's viewpoints, peddling disinformation about the MEK, discouraging U.S. officials from pursuing regime change, and warning against support for alternatives to the despotic regime, specifically the MEK.

In January 2020, Tabatabai remarked at a conference at Georgetown University, "What happens next if there is a collapse in the regime? Right, there are a bunch of different scenarios that can happen. Some of them are, some of them are more pleasant to think about such as you have the current regime topple and then you have a democratic sort of secular democracy replacing the regime."

"But, there are also several other scenarios that are more likely than that. And that's something else to take into account. So, yes, you could have a democracy that replaces the current regime and changes everything we've discussed. Stop supporting Hezbollah, stop sending troops to Iraq and Syria."

"There's also a world in which the next regime ends up being a different flavor of the current one. I'm thinking of a group like the MEK that has been around for decades. That is seen as a viable alternative by some circles in the city. But that in Iran is seen as an illegitimate force, precisely because of some of its history and activities in the past."[3]

Hindsight is 20/20 when it comes to counterintelligence but SEMAFOR's groundbreaking revelations notwithstanding, scholars have long understood that the targeting of pro-democracy movements the world over is best understood as a task undertaken by compromised individuals with often dubious motivations. Apologists for the Iranian regime – particularly those involved in the incessant demonization of the MEK – generally have a foot in Tehran.

Iran Experts Initiative (IEI)

According to public reporting, Tabatabai is one of the founding members of an influence operation called the Iran Experts Initiative (IEI). In a March 2014 letter to Mostafa Zahrani, the head of the Iranian regime's Foreign Ministry think tank in Tehran, an Iranian diplomat named Saeed Khatibzadeh wrote that he, Tabatabai, and another academic named Dina Esfandiary had "agreed to be the core group of the IEI" and had invited several other scholars to take part in a conference in Vienna while nuclear negotiations were ongoing in that same city.

Tabatabai traveled to Tehran in June 2014. Following the conference, the IEI members communicated in-depth and at length with Iranian officials and state-affiliated researchers, collaborating on op-eds and talking points and seeking advice about professional matters such as whether to attend a conference.

One month after the conference, Tabatabai contacted Zahrani about her dual invitations to events in Saudi Arabia and Israel and was told that the latter was "better to be avoided." According to SEMAFOR, which obtained these and thousands of other Iranian email communications, she seemingly took guidance from her regime handlers by following up with, "Thank you very much for your advice. I will take action regarding Saudi Arabia and keep you updated on the progress."

On other occasions, Tabatabai and fellow participants in the IEI reportedly submitted draft op-eds to their contacts in Iran, soliciting comments and requests for revision before publishing articles that effectively conveyed the viewpoint that the Islamic Republic intended to promote to deceive American policymakers.

These viewpoints included beliefs such as, "According to Khamenei's fatwa, Nuclear bomb is not Halal in Shiite belief and therefore will not be developed by the theocratic regime" and "the regime has no viable alternative and MEK is disliked in Iran, and therefore this regime has to and will stay despite any discontent." The aim was always to discourage a shift in the U.S. government toward a realistic regime change policy in Iran.

"Protests and discontents and reform efforts are all an inherent part of Iranian public life," Tabatabai remarked at a Georgetown University conference in January 2020. "Now the question to me is, does the regime manage to control this discontent? So far, the answer has been yes. If you go back to 2009, then later to 2012, then 2017, and then 2018, people have been predicting that the Islamic Republic will collapse. And, actually, there is a joke that goes around in Iranian families, which is, you know, 'Inshallah, next year in Tehran.' Right, but Inshallah, next year in Tehran has been sort of taking down the road for 41 years. And so we shouldn't be making policies based on what we hope will happen. We should be thinking about the political reality and dealing with that and making policies accordingly."[4]

While Tabatabai appears nothing like the average follower of Supreme Leader Khamenei, trying hard in her pre-government service years to maintain the appearance of a legitimate researcher, her public remarks have often served to reiterate what the regime's club-wielding hooligans tell students and protesters, namely "Demonstrations and protests will bear no fruit, the Islamic Republic is here to stay. Don't waste your time and life. Accept the reality as it is. Iran will never be free." Presuming that Iranian's yearning for freedom and a democratic republic is a "joke," she seems to conclude that Iranians should abandon hope for a brighter future by surrendering to the ayatollahs as opposed to closing ranks with the Iranian resistance.

In Tabatabai's view, Iranians are compulsive protesters and demonstrators. Pouring into the streets and crying out for civil and human rights is simply a normal part of everyday life, not indications of an overarching desire for change in Iran. "If we think of protests as an unusual thing in the Iranian life, then yes, we might think of what is going on here now as a big change. But protests are actually a feature of the Islamic Republic."

Tehran's protectors

After 15 months of service in the State Department, Tabatabai assumed the role of Chief of Staff to the Assistant Secretary of Defense for Special Operations and Low-Intensity Conflicts. After the revelations in SEMAFOR, U.S. Representatives Mike Rogers and Jack Bergman sent a letter to the Department of Defense demanding explanations for how Tabatabai received a security clearance given her allegedly close working relationship with the Iranian regime.

Other aspects of Tehran's influence operation have not been fully revealed to date, including a well-coordinated smear campaign directed at the regime's democratic opponents. To the extent that Tabatabai successfully gave lawmakers pause in their dealings with Tehran's democratic foes, there are grounds to challenge the integrity of many expert assessments that Iran's well-resourced lobby may have influenced.

Indeed, the growing awareness of these operations justifies a comprehensive reconsideration of Western policy toward the Islamic Republic and its democratic opponents. American and European officials should next determine who else may be implicated in collaborations with Iranian agents and identify the full extent of the damage caused.

U.S. Congress stands firm

On September 29, 2023, U.S. Senator Roger Wicker, R-Miss., ranking member of the Senate Armed Services Committee, led a letter[5] that was signed by 30 Senate Republicans[6] demanding a full accounting of actions taken by the senior Pentagon official Ariane Tabatabai.[7] The letter noted that Tabatabai maintained close links to the Iranian government while working as the chief of staff to the Assistant Secretary of Defense for Special Operations and Low Intensity Conflict.

The senators expressed concern that Tabatabai was allegedly engaged in an Iranian government-linked initiative to bolster the Iranian government's image and reinforce Tehran's national security views. The senators suggested that it is "unconscionable" for Tabatabai to continue holding a sensitive national defense-related position and called for the immediate suspension of her security clearance.[8]

In the U.S. House of Representatives, a separate letter signed by Representative Mike Rogers, Chairman of the House Committee on Armed Services, and Representative Jack Bergman, Chairman of the Subcommittee on Intelligence and Special Operations, expressed deep concern with the decision by the Department of Defense to hire Tabatabai. "Ms. Tabatabai's past employment history and close ties to the Iranian regime are alarming and should be disqualifying for anyone seeking such a sensitive position of trust within the United States Department of Defense," they stressed in the letter.

The representatives rightly asserted that as the world's leading state sponsor of terrorism, and as a clear adversary of the United States, the Iranian regime poses a direct national security threat to United States citizens and security interests and insisted that no person who aligns themselves with a hostile state or who acts as a foreign agent should wield influence over U.S. policy or have access to sensitive national security information.[9]

PART II

PRO-DEMOCRACY, ANTI-REGIME PROTESTS

Waves of social unrest rock the Islamic Republic of Iran

THE IRANIAN REGIME HAS BEEN HAMMERED by repeated waves of countrywide, anti-regime protests since September 2022. In that year alone, some 280 cities in all 31 provinces and many key universities and high schools participated in collective action against their rulers. Sparked by the regime's inhumane treatment of women, including the murder of 22-year-old Kurdish-Iranian Mahsa (Zhina) Amini, the people's remonstrations rapidly transformed into a democratic revolution and nearly universal calls for regime change.

The roots of the simmering dissent were, and are, deep. The Islamic Republic of Iran's economic portrait has long been bleak, with economic activity contracting at an alarming rate. In the first half of 2022, more than 750 people were killed in nationwide protests, including 60 women and upwards of 70 teenagers under the age of 18, and at least 30,000 people were arrested. The regime announced that dozens of its repressive forces, both uniformed and plainclothes, were killed in clashes, and hundreds of others were injured as Iranians took to the streets to defend themselves against brutal attacks.[10]

The discontent observable on the Iranian street continues to be extensive, with recent protests outliving all those since at least 2017, but it is hardly new. The country has a decades-long history of being crippled by extensive state corruption and misappropriation of funds.[11] Moreover, the lack of an economic strategy, coupled with general political mismanagement and corruption, have led to the destruction of the country's economic infrastructure. As a result, the Iranian people are increasingly restive. Over the past three years, public anger has morphed into widespread protests and countrywide social uprisings.[12] Iranian officials rightly fear more intense and long-lasting protests that could have devastating consequences for the ruling elite, not unlike the overthrow of dictatorships in the past.

Officials are therefore increasingly weary of the activities of opponents who have the capacity to lead and guide protests toward genuine democratic change. The regime's highest authority, supreme leader Ali Khamenei, voiced this unease in the context of the attraction of young people to the main opposition movement, the Mujahedin-e Khalq (MEK). He said: "There are actually two big detriments jeopardizing youth environments: one is passivity, and another is deviation [a frequent reference to the MEK]… Everyone should pay attention that they too are working on our youth. They are trying to take advantage of our youth. Everyone should pay attention and take care not to help the enemy recruit the youth of the country."[13]

As a result, Iran's government has drastically stepped up its influence operations and disinformation machine against major opponents threatening its declining status. Nowhere is this better illustrated than its evolving treatment of the main opposition movement, the People's Mojahedin Organization of Iran (PMOI)[14], also known as Mujahedeen-e Khalq (MEK). The 57-year-old MEK has long been deemed Tehran's most potent existential threat by virtue of its organizational prowess,[15] intelligence-gathering capabilities,[16] financial resources,[17] dedicated ranks,[18] and a significant domestic following and network of supporters.[19]

Meanwhile, internationally, the MEK has scored substantial political backing from lawmakers in the U.S., parliamentarians in Europe, and global luminaries, intellectuals, and senior former western government officials. In July 2019, a large bi-partisan American delegation visited thousands of MEK activists in Albania. According to a subsequent report, they witnessed a cohesive political movement, guided by a female and gifted leadership, with a well-defined political platform and a vast network of passionate supporters inside Iran and across the world eager to implement it.[20]

In these critical times for Tehran, Iranian policymakers may operate under the assumption that the potency and range of the MEK's social penetration has dramatically increased.[21] The range of sociopolitical actors dissatisfied with the status quo and potentially gravitating toward an alternative like the MEK is expanding by the day.[22] Making matters worse for the ayatollahs, the MEK, with its allies in the coalition of the NCRI, seem to offer, at least for now, the only realistic political alternative due to its organized network, political experience and social backing.[23] One would be pressed to find a single collective in the constellation of Iranian opponents that even approaches the influence wielded by the MEK across a variety of critical analytical dimensions.[24] That distinction, however, leaves a significant target on its back.

In addition to using state-run radio stations, TV networks, websites, and other media outlets to demonize the MEK, the Iranian government has also stepped up the production of its movies, TV series, documentaries, articles, books, exhibitions, and other public relations instruments. Some of the key tactics are outlined in this book.[25]

The strategic policy of the Islamic Republic's supreme leader, Ali Khamenei, against the MEK is rooted in the familiar range of maximalist and minimalist expectations. The top maximalist band seeks total physical annihilation of the organization, or perhaps more importantly politically destroying the organization through delegitimizing it.[26] The minimalist point seeks to at least neutralize or severely curb the MEK's influence or social pull. That is why Iranian government agencies are using not only propaganda (minimalist) but also terrorism and physical annihilation tactics (maximalist) as a dual-track policy to achieve their core objectives. In the end, the elimination of the MEK, in the eyes of authorities, would significantly shift the balance of power in their favor, by effectively removing any popular desire to pay the requisite price for change. In the absence of a real political alternative, why rise and risk imprisonment or death?

A review of Tehran's conduct shows that intelligence and security agencies are using a variety of domestic and international resources to implement their plans. This includes spending exorbitant sums of money to execute public relations objectives against the MEK.[27]

How Tehran has decided to deal with this formidable political adversary affords important lessons about the ruling elite's perception of its opposition, how it uses disinformation to discredit and dehumanize opponents, and the depth and breadth of the MEK's popularity inside the country. The latter metric is critically important because it shows how the country's widespread discontent is being channeled into an existing political structure with the purported ability to change the status quo. It is almost universally acknowledged that there is no appetite to remove the fundamentalist regime from power through direct Western involvement. Yet the regime's threats cannot be ignored. That is why an organized democratic opposition presents a critical component for the West's Iran policy. Tehran's attempts to manipulate Western opinion about this organization must be countered effectively. Additionally, recognition by the United States and the international community of the right of the Iranian people to self-defense and to overthrow the regime is long overdue.

The MEK's threat to a fundamentalist regime

The recent protests in Iran have been blamed by regime officials on the main opposition Mujahedin-e Khalq (MEK). On November 5, 2022, for example, the regime Supreme Leader Ali Khamenei's main representative in the Islamic Revolutionary Guard Corps (IRGC), said that close to 50 main leaders of the recent protesters detained were members of the MEK.[28] Officials in various provinces have also pointed the finger at the MEK for organizing the anti-regime rallies. The commander of the Lorestan province State Security Forces (SSF), for example, was quoted by a state news agency as saying that the regime has discovered from mass arrests that many are members of the MEK.[29]

As for the MEK's increasing appeal among the youth, Hossein Sazvar, a state-affiliated propagandist, told the state-run Ofogh TV on November 5, "Yesterday, one of my friends told me something which left me in pain. He said he met one of these rioters on the streets and asked him whether he hated the Islamic Republic more or the hypocrites (the pejorative term the regime uses to refer to the MEK). The guy responded to my friend, 'first of all, their name is not the hypocrites. It's called the Mujahedin-e Khalq (MEK). Secondly, what have they done?'"[30]

During his Friday prayer sermon, Mohammad-Hossein Hosseini Hamedani, Khamenei's representative in Alborz province, said: "The rioters' case is completely different. They should be dealt with firmly, as they have disrupted society. They are repeating the same norm-breaking actions the MEK undertook in the 1980s. We never forgive nor forget the MEK."

These are not isolated cases. on May 5, 2020, in a telling development that stands out among many similar cases, Iran's judiciary spokesman acknowledged the earlier arrest of two accomplished university students. They were charged with having ties to the MEK.[31] The students, Ali Younesi and Amir Hossein Moradi, studied at the equivalent of the American MIT in Iran (Sharif University of Technology) and were intelligent scholars that had won competitive global and national prizes in astronomy and astrophysics.[32] Simultaneously, the organization announced on May 5, 2020 the names of 18 others it said had been recently arrested as well.[33] Nearly half were women, displaying the apparent popularity of the organization among young Iranian women eager for change in Iran. The MEK is the pivotal force within the coalition of the National Council of Resistance of Iran (NCRI) and it is led by a woman, Maryam Rajavi, who is frequently vilified by the mullahs for her efforts to advance gender equality in the country.[34]

The arrests served as yet another reminder that, not only does the MEK remain relevant to successive generations of Iranians in spite of harsh controls on the flow of information, it is increasingly considered by the authorities to be an existential threat.[35] Intellectuals and students continue to gravitate toward the organization's message, its perceived dedication to democracy, and its general staying power in the face of brutal tactics employed by the state over the years.[36] In May 2019, the MEK published the names of another 39 of its supporters arrested by the government. At the time, the creation of its "Resistance Units" had grabbed domestic attention.[37]

Then-Intelligence Minister Mahmoud Alavi said on April 19, 2019, "Over the past year, 116 teams ("Resistance Units" in MEK parlance) associated with the MEK have been dealt with."[38] And, in May 2019, Tehran's "revolutionary" court sentenced MEK activist Abdullah Ghassempour, 34, to death, while sentencing several others to imprisonment on charges of supporting the MEK.[39]

Against that backdrop, Tehran seems to be scrambling to execute a policy of demonization, propaganda and, at times, deadly terrorism against the MEK.[40] Major social uprisings broke out in December 2017, November 2019, and September 2022, which were more organized and politically sophisticated, causing the regime to draw the conclusion that the MEK was involved in leading the mass protests;[41] and finally, U.S. policy shifted away from seeking rapprochement vis-à-vis Tehran, laying the groundwork for further international pressure on the Iranian government.

The message of the 2022 protests to the world is impressively unified and is focused on the overthrow of the regime. The most universal slogan is "Death to dictator, death to Khamenei." Other dominant slogans all target the heart of the regime, seeking to unseat the Ayatollahs, while rejecting the past single-party rule of the Shah, as in the chant "Death to the oppressor, be it the Shah or the Leader [Khamenei]." What is happening in Iran has all the hallmarks of a revolution in the making.

During the 2018 uprisings, an official of the Islamic Revolutionary Guard Corps (IRGC), now on the U.S. list of terrorist organizations, said: "As an expert, I say the grouplet of Monafeqin-hypocrisy (the regime's disparaging term to describe the MEK) and essentially the MEK brand is not dying or disappearing. Anyone who says that the hypocrites are dead is either wrong or ignorant; wrong in the sense that if he is not the enemy himself and does not have animosity toward the Islamic Republic system, he is an accessory; and ignorant in the sense that he is simply unaware."[42]

To neutralize or at least limit the MEK's social infiltration, especially among the youth, as mentioned above, Iranian officials have allocated significant funding to advance a well-oiled and sophisticated campaign of attacking the MEK.[43] Among the tools used are a colorful array of networks, agents, media outlets, and allies to spread false information against the organization, its members and especially its leaders.[44]

Iran's objective for escalating these propaganda efforts seems to be two-fold: First, propaganda dehumanizes the target, and lays the groundwork to suppress, imprison, torture, or physically destroy MEK dissidents without – the government hopes – triggering widespread social backlash or severe political costs; and second, such propaganda conveys to western interlocutors that the MEK, which claims to be calling for a free Iran, is even worse than the current theocratic state. Therefore, the argument goes, the status quo has no alternative, and a coherent *realpolitik* outlook dictates that the current government should be preserved, accommodated, and even appeased.

Taking a page from Hitler's playbook

Demonizing one's adversary and spreading propaganda is a well-known tactic in psychological warfare. The Iranian government's employment of influence operations, and specifically its use of propaganda in the 21st century, including an array of tactics,[45] has historical parallels. The Office of Strategic Services (OSS) – a wartime intelligence agency in the United States during World War II, and a predecessor to the Central Intelligence

Agency (CIA) – was tasked with developing precise assessments of the conduct and behaviors of Nazi leader Adolf Hitler.⁴⁶

The agency delegated this responsibility to Walter C. Langer, a proficient psychologist. In 1943, Langer released a 170-page report on Hitler's personality entitled "A Psychological Analysis of Adolph Hitler: His Life and Legend." The report was later declassified from the CIA archives.⁴⁷

The report states: "His primary rules were: never allow the public to cool off; never admit a fault or wrong; never concede that there may be some good in your enemy; never leave room for alternatives; never accept blame; concentrate on one enemy at a time and blame him for everything that goes wrong; people will believe a big lie sooner than a little one; and if you repeat it frequently enough, people will sooner or later believe it."⁴⁸

Langer prepared the report based on Hitler's tactics, thinking, and writings. Hitler had previously espoused his "big lies" philosophy. In the second section of his book *Mein Kampf* ("My Struggle"), Hitler writes in chapter 11, Propaganda and Organization:

- ❖ The first task of propaganda is to create individuals who can form future organizations.
- ❖ The second task of propaganda is to uproot public assumptions and recreate new ones.
- ❖ Propaganda comes before all else because others' opinions must be shaped by our propaganda.
- ❖ One must use propaganda for a specific period to instill a dominant opinion amongst the public.
- ❖ Propaganda must infuse new thinking and philosophy among the masses; and
- ❖ All political movements must shake up the status quo and propaganda instruments must gradually infuse their method of thinking into the mindset of the masses.⁴⁹

Hitler's outlook on propaganda can hardly be distinguished from that employed by the Iranian regime.

Today, the Iranian government is internationally rebuked for egregious human rights violations and its embrace of malign foreign policies long admonished by Western governments.[50] One could argue that these policies have paved the way for the near destruction of Iran as a functioning nation-state. The price of the status quo will be severe, but the clerical elites are keen to preserve their power. It appears that to do this, they must engage in the wholesale discrediting and delegitimization of their opponents, chief among them the MEK.

This report covers the Iranian government's domestic influence operations against the MEK in three sections:

1. The Iranian officials' multifaceted soft war against the organization, including the production of TV series, movies, and books to shape the desired social narrative.

2. A review of the security and intelligence agencies behind this effort; and

3. The motivation underpinning the regime's decision to increase its operations against the MEK within the context of deepening anti-government sentiment.

PART III

DISINFORMATION AND INFLUENCE OPERATIONS

SOME OF THE KEY ASPECTS OF THE IRANIAN REGIME'S PROPAGANDA CAMPAIGN against its principal opponents in the Mujahedin-e Khalq (MEK) are not new. Tehran's influence operations have a long history because the MEK has been viewed as the best organized and most potent opposition to the regime for more than forty years and because the organization's efforts, actions, and policies have had a defining impact on the evolution of the state's restructuring since 1979. Its actions and positions have also significantly influenced the clerical government's national security and intelligence considerations.[51] One of the regime's prominent analysts, who teaches at Beheshti University, said in 2019: "The MEK in the past 40 years, if we consider the overall impact, they have inflicted the most harm against the Islamic Republic. ... At any rate, they are organized. There is no other organized force completely devoted against the Islamic Republic system. Currently, there may be many MEK supporters in the country and they collect information."[52]

The clash between the two adversaries began in earnest in the aftermath of the anti-monarchic revolution of February 1979. Once the clerics took power, the MEK was the first major party to condemn their move to establish the *velayat-e faqih* (absolute clerical rule) principle in the new constitution.⁵³ The clerics were swift to move in to silence the organization and prevent its political rationale to seep deeper into the broader society. Attacks were made on MEK rallies and their campaign offices. It is estimated that at least 71 MEK members were killed by the regime and thousands imprisoned from February 1979 to June 1981, even though the organization had committed to peacefully participate in the political process.⁵⁴

Later, the MEK became the most vociferous voice for peace during the eight-year Iran-Iraq war, ⁵⁵ which irritated a government that had made huge investments in the war effort and to project its power regionally. The regime retaliated against the organization by massacring thousands of its supporters still in prisons across Iran in 1988. The bloody episode, which to this day haunts the psyche of Iranian society, has been condemned by Amnesty International as a "crime against humanity."⁵⁶

In 2002, the MEK became the first actor to expose Iran's clandestine nuclear weapons program, triggering international sanctions and isolation for the regime.⁵⁷ The MEK has also waged an international campaign to highlight the government's human rights abuses and its support for terrorism, which has led to a long list of condemnations by parliaments, human rights organizations, the United Nations, and governments across the world.⁵⁸ The organization has more recently become the leading voice of protests and social uprisings in Iran, prompting senior officials to publicly express worries in unprecedented ways.⁵⁹ These activities and others have turned the MEK into the most serious challenge to Tehran, causing the state to counter its role through propaganda and demonization.

The early years of government propaganda against the MEK can be described as largely unsophisticated, and limited primarily to the dissemination of rumors, fake stories, lies and accusations. But, over time and in lockstep with the rapid evolution of social developments and associated complexities, the government's approach became more complex and refined, and more potent too.

Although exact figures are not known because of lack of budgetary transparency, Tehran has spent substantial money on anti-MEK propaganda to pursue the following objectives: Distort and twist the MEK's long and complex history, fabricate inaccurate and false narratives about the organization's internal arrangements, demonize the MEK publicly, downplay its organizational prowess, turn the tide of public opinion against it by generally discrediting the organization's policies, and shape public opinion in a way that would be hostile to the MEK's leaders in particular.[60] Discrediting the leadership and the MEK's brand saves the government the pain of discrediting individual rank-and-file, granting it the potential leeway to recruit defectors in order to use them for various intelligence and terrorist operations.[61]

Initiatives and campaigns that have been executed by the government to deliver on its anti-MEK propaganda agenda are listed in this report (starting in March 2019). Since the MEK is at the epicenter of opposition to the Iranian state, officials may be employing a broader strategy in the hopes that the MEK's marginalization will render the entire idea of opposition to the ayatollahs futile. How successful Tehran will be in this effort remains to be seen. Certainly, in the past 42 years, the regime has not been able to annihilate the organization.

Production of movies and TV series defacing the MEK

After the November 2019 uprising in at least 200 cities, during which security forces gunned down over 1,500 protestors in a matter of two weeks,[62] the Iranian government began mass production and distribution of state-affiliated movies, TV series, and documentaries, including obtaining forced confessions from detainees, against the uprising and specifically the MEK. Various state officials, including supreme leader Ali Khamenei, have pointed to the MEK as the leader and instigator of the uprisings.[63] The government also aired programming about the anniversary of the 2009 protests.[64] All this poses the question: Why is the Iranian government so intensely focused on such deliberate efforts to ruin the MEK's reputation?

The state's security-focused approach, aimed at curbing further protests, includes guidelines prescribed by Tehran's intelligence ministry (officially known as the Ministry of Intelligence and Security, or MOIS) and its judiciary.[65]

Since 2017, and especially after massive national uprisings were triggered, to the end of December 2019, various state-run TV networks aired at least 10 documentaries and a long TV series bashing the MEK.[66] One of the recent documentaries is called "Sarcheshmeh" (The Origin). Its first season has 20 episodes that are 50 minutes long each.[67] In other words, more than 1,000 minutes of public programming are contained in this single instance.

The documentaries broadcast on various channels inside Iran use the intelligence ministry's oft-repeated tactic of obtaining forced confessions. The titles of some of these state-produced movies, documentaries, and TV series over just the past two years include:

1. Sarcheshmeh ("The Origin" – TV series)
2. Terror (documentary)
3. The Mujahedin-e Khalq Organization after 50 years (documentary)
4. Khab-e Ashofteh ("A Turbulent Sleep" – documentary)
5. Nofouzi ("The Mole" – documentary)
6. Be Nam-e Khalq ("In the Name of the People" – documentary, 29 episodes)
7. Gorgha dar Kamin ("Wolves in Ambush" – documentary)
8. Khial-e Kham ("Wishful Thinking" – documentary)
9. Payan-e Rah ("End of the Road" – documentary)
10. Shahrag ("The Jugular" – TV series, 30 episodes)
11. Khesht-e Khasm ("The Brick of Hostility" – documentary, 5 episodes)

12. Sazman ("The Organization" – documentary)
13. Qabilian (documentary)
14. Radd-e Pay-e Gorgha ("The Wolves' Tracks" – documentary)
15. Sazman-e Terror ("The Organization of Terror" – documentary)
16. Meh Shekan ("Fog Light" – documentary, 40+ episodes)
17. Anche Gozasht ("What Happened" – documentary)
18. Qabrhay-e Por Sar-o-Seda ("The Piercing Sounds of Graves" – documentary)
19. Shohaday-e Terror ("Martyrs of Terrorism" – documentary)

Authorities have arranged to produce many other movies and television slots to deface and discredit the MEK's public image.[68] State-affiliated figures pose as directors, TV producers, or screenwriters, but they toe the line of the MOIS.[69]

In 2020, the government rolled out its annual Fajr Film Festival (February 11 to February 21). State-run media reported in February: "After the conclusion of the Fajr Film Festival and based on an overall scanning of the movies that were screened, one can clearly see that the movement of directors in recent years toward security-focused films has seen a marked rise."[70]

The report adds: "In recent years, works with security, historical and political themes have received the Simorgh (highest award). These include: 'Midday Adventures,' 'Trace of Blood,' and others, which are clear examples of this trend."[71] Both features mentioned are considered propaganda films against the MEK.

Publication of books against the MEK

Eight anti-MEK books have also recently been published as part of the propaganda war against the opposition movement:

1. **Strategy and Nothing Else**, written by Mohammad-Hassan Rouzi Talab, published by Ya Zahra Publications, 246 pages.

2. **Raid against Bats**, written by Mohammad Sattari Vafai, published by Shahid Kazemi publications. This book contains several declassified documents by the protection office of the MOIS from the early 1980s.

3. **A Credible Narrative about the MEK**, written by Shahram Bozorgi, published by Astan-e Qods Razavi, 83 pages. This book reviews and analyzes the MEK in recent years and more recent developments, including its behavior and conduct.

4. **Bahman Bazargani: Interviews, memories, and analytical articles about the MEK, the leftist movement and the Islamic Revolution**, published by Nashr-e Ney publications, 217 pages. This book contains a memoir from Bahman Bazargani from the 1970s.

5. **The Days of Being an Heir Apparent: A review of historical documents showing relations between Ayatollah Montazeri and the MEK**, published by the Islamic Revolution Historical Studies and Encyclopedia Foundation, 450 pages. Montazeri was heir apparent to Khomeini, the regime's first supreme leader, but was deposed after he criticized the massacre of MEK political prisoners by authorities in 1988.

6. **Between Two Worlds**: Memoirs of Ali Bakhsh Afaridandeh (Reza Gouran), published by Pezhvak-e Iran, 724 pages, March 12, 2020. The author is an MOIS agent.

7. **The Savior Newsletter**, which is published on the Nejat (Savior) Foundation English website.

8. **The Untold Stories of Guerilla Warfare**, written by Mohammad Hassan Rouzi Talab, 348 pages. This book reviews purported documents and evidence from the 1980s with respect to the regime's urban conflict against the MEK.

The covers of "A Credible Narrative about the MEK" and "Raid against the bats"

The Cover of "Bahman Bazargani: Interviews..."

The Covers of "Strategy and Nothing Else" and "Between Two Worlds"

PART IV

SECURITY AGENCIES ACTIVE AGAINST THE MEK

THERE IS AT LEAST ONE CENTRAL QUESTION that comes to mind after reviewing these productions against the MEK: What institutions or organs produce and distribute these movies, TV series, documentaries, and publications inside and outside Iran? Are they normal cultural institutions as seen in other countries or are they something else? A review of two of the most active "behind the scenes" entities sheds light on the matter.

Owj Arts and Media Organization

Established in 2011, the Owj ("Summit") Arts and Media Organization is tied to the cultural affairs section of the Islamic Revolutionary Guard Corps (IRGC).[72] The organization grew from the government's political conclusions about the 2009 uprising.[73] Based on their analysis of the

2009 protests, Tehran's authorities adopted several specific measures to effectively confront potential uprisings in the future:

1. The status of the intelligence office of the IRGC was elevated and it became the Intelligence Organization. This organ plays the same role that the Third Bureau of the former Shah's secret police SAVAK did (before 1979) in identifying and suppressing dissidents. The Bassij paramilitary and various plainclothes agent organizations were regrouped as the operational and executive arms of the IRGC's Intelligence Organization.[74]

2. The cultural affairs office of the IRGC expanded its apparatus in alignment with the security and intelligence organs above to wage psychological warfare targeting youth. It aims to infuse reactionary ideologies and thinking into young people's mainstream ideas. By the end of 2016, the former commander of Bassij, Brig. Gen. Mohammad-Reza Naqdi, was transferred to lead the IRGC's cultural affairs office.[75]

3. In 2011, the IRGC's cultural affairs office created the Owj media organization to execute the office's objectives. The organization

The head of Owj media organization, Ehsan Mohammad Hassani, attending the swearing in ceremony of the IRGC's commander-in-chief, April 2019.

is headed by Ehsan Mohammad Hassani, who is also in close contact with the *Ammarioun Base*, which organizes state-affiliated plainclothes agents. He is supported financially by the former State Security Forces (SSF) Commander and mayor of Tehran, Brig. Gen. Mohammad Baqer Qalibaf. Qalibaf is currently the Parliament Speaker.[76]

The causes of establishing Owj

The establishment of what government agencies describe as "culture and arts" institutions like Owj is a reflection of the growing recognition by supreme leader Ali Khamenei, the IRGC, and other security and military establishment players that their social base inside Iran is dwindling.[77] Deeply concerned about popular uprisings, their efforts are intended to legitimize their unstable rule in any way they can by justifying four decades of massacres, suppression, murder, and other crimes.[78] At the same time, such entities are created to produce movies and documentaries, while spending large sums of money in other avenues, to confront the MEK through psychological warfare.

Financial sources of Owj

According to its officials, Owj obtains its funding from the IRGC. In August 2017, the head of the Owj organization, Ehsan Mohammad Hassani, said in an interview in response to a question about the organization's budgets and financial support: "The Owj organization is proud that it does not receive any money from a foreign embassy and that it proudly obtains support from the IRGC."[79]

In November 2014, the head of the IRGC's public relations office, Brig. Gen. Ramezan Sharif, said in a press briefing: "Since the very beginning, the Owj organization declared a clear orientation toward being active in the areas of Revolution [establishment of the clerical regime], the Sacred Defense [Iran-Iraq war] and the Islamic Awakening [the regime's spread of fundamentalism in the region]. All three areas have a close connection with the IRGC's activities. In that respect, the organization's activities would not have been possible without a close-knit cooperation and support from institutions like the IRGC and the armed forces."[80]

What is Owj's mandate?

The IRGC has increased its active involvement in media and cultural affairs. With the establishment of Owj, the IRGC intends to fill the vacuum left by some former active state organs in the propaganda and soft war campaigns.[81] It is eager to quickly expand its activities even beyond the state-run TV and radio broadcasters.[82]

Under the guise of producing movies and documentaries, Owj implements projects designed by IRGC and other intelligence and security organs against the opposition MEK.[83] According to internal statements made by some of Owj's officials,[84] the organization executes IRGC and Bassij paramilitary propaganda projects, controls over 80 other institutions and subsidiaries, employs at least 2,600 people, and produces about 700 documentaries a year through one of its subsidiaries called Khan-e Tarrahan Enghelab Eslami ("The House of Designers of the Islamic Revolution").[85]

Not surprisingly, the movies and documentaries produced by Owj portray the IRGC's suppressive policies and actions as justified and legitimate.

Other topics presented in a favorable light in these productions include the nuclear weapons program and foreign meddling, including what the international community has described as government-sponsored terrorism.[86]

The decisionmakers

Ali Qanavati, head of the Sooreh television organization and former director of the Oil Ministry's public relations office, has talked about the Owj organization's activities within the state-run media. He wrote on February 14, 2018: "The television department of Owj is a completely different story. Here, too, the chairman of the organization, much like the current head of state-run TV and radio broadcaster, is not involved in the decision-making process and his presence is largely ceremonial. So, who is the main decision maker? ... The majority of the names, projects, and subsidiaries that we witness point to one thing: In the majority of Owj television activities, there is a pronounced presence of a senior member of the country's security apparatus, who is rarely identified as such. In his rare media appearances, he introduces himself as an expert in cultural or media relations or a university professor. His security expertise is much more than his understanding of an insignificant media outlet."[87]

It is reasonable to conclude that the type of individual mentioned in such statements is a senior security official in the IRGC's intelligence organization or in the MOIS (the regime's intelligence ministry). It is also quite evident from such statements that directors and producers of anti-MEK movies and TV series are closely aligned with these officials.[88]

In the movie "Midday Adventures," directed by Mohammad Hossein Mahdavian, the credits refer to a curious "adviser" identified as "Morteza Esfahani."[89] Farhad Towhidi, born in the northern city of Rasht, is a screenwriter who worked on the screenplay for the anti-MEK movie

"Emkan-e Mina" (Mina's Choice).[90] In an interview with Iran Wire on May 22, 2018, Towhidi says the following about "Esfahani":

> "My information about this person is minimal, much like yours. I worked with him for a very brief and limited period. He told me that he produces documentaries, but I did not ask which ones. In our limited interactions, our focus was on the information that he would provide us regarding the specific locations and times of events and conflicts between the MEK and the intelligence ministry. Regarding his honesty, it is natural that we do not have access to the other side's information, and we don't know what the other side [MEK] says. I think as someone who gave us intelligence and had a political stance regarding the MEK, his narrative did not conflict with the statements of those who have defected from the organization and have written memoirs and are critical of the MEK today. The defection of those people from the MEK perhaps happened with the help that he [Esfahani] and his colleagues provided, but we did not notice any contradictions in the narratives. One day, Mr. Esfahani brought one of these defectors from the MEK to the production stage. This person gave me what I needed, such as information about safe houses. (Esfahani) had given us valuable information for the Mina's Choice project. Mr. Manouchehr Mohammadi had thought about the main idea for the script. Kamal Tabrizi was also with him. They both proposed the idea to me. When the contract was signed, they introduced me to Mr. Esfahani so he could help as a 'security adviser' and provide some information to me as I wrote the screenplay. It appeared to me that he was a retired intelligence agent and during his service he had worked on the MEK dossier. Prior to the engagement, he had also provided consultation to various TV series regarding this topic. At any rate, he contributed to the writing of the screenplay, especially the ending of the movie, which was modified based on his views. Talking about the issues of the 1980s is not very simple and the presence of people like Mr. Esfahani provided the opportunity to do so."[91]

Who is "Esfahani"?

Morteza Ghobbeh, also known as Esfahani, is reportedly a veteran Iranian intelligence operative with decades of experience in this field.[92] According to Radio Farda, "Esfahani, whose real name is Morteza Ghobbeh, is still actively involved in filmmaking for Iran's intelligence organizations... All of these movies propagate the Islamic Republic's official narrative about certain events such as espionage and the way the Islamic Republic treated the opposition group Mojahedin-e Khalq (MeK)."[93] Esfahani himself said in an interview with Sobh-e No: "I am a fighter for the Islamic Republic. I learned at the intelligence operations of the asymmetric warfare headquarters how important the role of intelligence is on the frontlines."[94] He reportedly worked closely with another notorious intelligence operative, then-deputy Intelligence Minister Saeed Emami, who was one of the figures involved in a series of gruesome murders of dissidents and intellectuals in 1998.[95] The bloody episode later became known as the "Chain Murders" scandal.[96] When the intelligence ministry's role became evident in the killings, drawing a vast public outcry, the regime apparently used Saeed Emami and his associates as sacrificial lamb and begrudgingly arrested them.[97]

After the Chain Murders dust settled – it was left inconclusive like so many so-called investigations of the regime's corruption and crimes dossiers – Esfahani once again returned to his intelligence activities in the regime's security apparatus.[98]

He is now considered a well-known adviser in state cinema for movies that have security-related, police, and espionage themes.[99] During his involvement in the production of state-sponsored movies and TV series, Esfahani likely acted as a security consultant to ensure that the content of these productions aligned with the preferred narratives of the government's intelligence services against the MEK.[100]

The names of "Esfahani" or "Morteza Ghobbeh" can be seen in the closing credits of various movies, documentaries, and TV series. They are accompanied by various titles, including consultant, quality manager, researcher, screenplay adviser, script doctor, screenplay consultant, consultant to the director, content consultant, or production consultant.

A video capture of Morteza Ghobbeh, also known as "Esfahani," who was interrogated in the aftermath of the 1990s Chain Murders scandal.

Morteza Ghobbeh, "Esfahani," pictured here in color, talking behind the scenes at the filming of the TV series "The Inverted Interpretation of a Dream."

These titles are put forward by security and intelligence organizations to mask the true role of these types of security personnel.

Some of Esfahani's key cinematic contributions are as follows:

1. Security consultant for the Midday Adventures 1 and 2 movies, directed by Mahdavian

2. Worked on the movie Cyanide, directed by Behrouz Shoeybi

3. Worked on the movie Mina's Choice, directed by Kamal Tabrizi

The movie Midday Adventures paints a sinister picture of the MEK and is one of the most well-known government attempts to demonize the organization on the big screen.[101] In July 2017, no less of an official than supreme leader Khamenei said about the movie: "This film, Midday Adventures, is really well done. All the movie's elements were excellent. The directing was excellent. The acting was excellent. The plot was excellent. The movie was well done."[102] Many of these types of movies have been produced by Owj media organization.[103]

The Ofogh TV Network

The Ofogh TV network was launched on June 3, 2014, as a test airing.[104] It was officially established on February 27, 2015, and currently, broadcasts programming 24 hours a day.[105] Ofogh is affiliated with Owj media organization, which produces a large portion of the network's content. The current director of Ofogh, Jalal Ghaffari, is a former dean of Social and Cultural Sciences department of Imam Hossein University, which is controlled by the IRGC.[106]

Jalal Ghaffari

Ofogh TV primarily focuses on cultural programming and attempts to offer diverse but specialized content in the areas of "Islamic Revolution," the Iran-Iraq war, "Islamic Awakening" (fundamentalism in the region), and an "Iranian-Islamic lifestyle."[107] It finances, produces, and airs these types of programming in various forms and styles.[108] The financial budget and personnel of this network are directly provided and appointed by IRGC organs.[109]

One of the network's focus areas is the demonization of the MEK, including distorting its past and history.[110] The network's studio guests, billed as "experts," are handpicked from factions and forces tied to Khamenei and the IRGC. Live "debate" programs, including one called "Jahan-e Ara" (World of Ideas), are the primary forums for the regime's intelligence apparatus to air anti-MEK content.[111]

PART V

FROM SILENCE TO ATTACKS

FOR A LONG TIME, the official policy of the Iranian government, the MOIS, and its media outlets was to be publicly silent about the MEK.[112] The aim was to attempt to erase the name and existence of the MEK in the eyes and minds of younger generations. However, especially after the 2009 uprisings, the regime discovered that the MEK's popularity and political significance continued to grow inside Iran, and the policy of silence was deemed detrimental to Tehran. In response, the regime unleashed a fierce and unrelenting propaganda broadside against the MEK.

On August 6, 2019, Javan daily, which is affiliated with the IRGC, published an article entitled "The MEK in Cinema." Javan wrote: "... For more than two decades, cinema had gone into a heavy silence and coma with respect to the MEK. Whether it wanted it or not, cinema had remained quiet about the topic. ... In the mid-2010s, however, an apparent revolution took place and a big development unfolded. The cinema started focusing directly and without any ambiguities on the MEK."[113]

The screenwriter of the state-sponsored documentary "In the Name of the People," Hamed Ghoreishi, who has also produced another documentary called "Former Soldier" against the MEK for the state-run foreign TV network Press TV, was asked about the motivation to produce such works. In response, he pointed to the "MEK's activities on the internet and attracting teenagers."[114]

Iman Goudarzi is another producer of documentaries proposed by Iran's intelligence ministry against the MEK. In December 2018, in an interview with IRGC-affiliated Javan daily, he explained the main reason for focusing on the MEK as such: "One of the things that forces us to turn to the issue of the MEK revolved around the events that occurred during the 2017 presidential elections. Some of the rival candidates pointed to conversations around the 1988 executions to switch the roles of martyr and executioner, as the Leader of the Revolution [Khamenei] pointed out."[115] The 1988 executions refer to the massacre of over 30,000 political prisoners, the overwhelming majority of whom were members and supporters of the MEK, based on a fatwa by the clerical state's founder, Ruhollah Khomeini.[116]

The MEK's influence

Evidence suggests that a series of events unfolded in 2016 that intensified the Iranian government's need to propagate more falsehoods against the MEK. A momentous development involved the collective relocation of MEK members to Albania and Europe from Iraq in 2016.[117] One of the first consequences of this relocation out of harm's way in Iraq and into safety was that the MEK could now more freely undertake events like those that unfolded in 2017 during Iran's presidential contest. At the time, questions swirled around the 1988 massacre, defeating the government's decades-old attempts to cover up the massacre as an official policy.[118] University students began to question the massacre publicly, something that had been unprecedented, and bore the risk of arrest and imprisonment. It was after these events that the clerical government sought to limit the growing popularity of the MEK more forcefully among younger generations. It thus intensified its campaign to vilify and demonize the MEK to historically justify the 1988 massacre. If the MEK could be portrayed as "terrorists" and "traitors," then killing them would not look as bad, the theory went. Still, both the policy of silence and subsequent attempts at ramped up vilification seem to have failed to produce the desired outcome, leaving the government little choice but to double down and drastically increase its requests to produce more anti-MEK movies and TV content to distribute its propaganda on a much larger scale.

The threat of overthrow and a "tsunami of fear"

The website Habilian is among a long list of online content producers tied to the intelligence ministry, MOIS. On July 22, 2019, the organization that runs the website launched a series of exhibitions against the MEK across Iran.[119] The statement released by the organizers declared: "The exhibition that shows pictures and documents related to the Mersad Operation (against the MEK in 1988) will be launched by the Organization of Documents and Evidence of the Sacred Defense [Iran-Iraq war] on July 27 and will last for a week at the National Archives headquarters. This exhibition will simultaneously be rolled out in the main provincial buildings of the Foundation for Preservation of Works and Values of the Sacred Defense in 31 provinces. Based on this report, on the sidelines of this exhibition, 25 books on the Sacred Defense will be unveiled."[120]

In 2019, on the anniversary of the Eternal Light Operation by the MEK, when the movement advanced 100 miles into Iranian territory in 1988, the government tried its utmost to shape public opinion by setting up various exhibitions and events all over Iran.[121]

The most senior-ranking officials of the Iranian government have publicly raised alarm over the MEK. IRGC general Gholamreza Jalali, head of Civil Defense Organization, told the state-run ISNA news agency on July 29, 2019: "In my view, the new war against the MEK in cyberspace is more difficult than the Mersad (Eternal Light) Operation [military confrontation]. ... The MEK is trying to exploit some domestic economic weaknesses and has issued an order for popular rebellion."[122]

The government spokesman for former President Hassan Rouhani, Ali Rabii, seemed to describe Tehran's fear of the MEK at a press briefing on July 28 and said: "Incidentally, I was thinking about how similar today's situation is with the Mersad days in several respects. I truly think that we are standing at the Charzebar Pass today [where the regime's forces and MEK faced off in 1988]. These days bear a striking resemblance to Mersad, and the MEK is behind the character assassination of the establishment's main personalities."[123]

Mostafa Pourmohammadi, a former member of the 1988 "death commission" responsible for the massacre of an estimated 30,000 MEK supporters,[124] who was also the justice minister during Rouhani's first term, told the Mosallas (Triangle) publication on July 25, 2019: "We have not yet settled the score with the MEK. We will discuss these matters after we eliminate them. ... Today, the MEK are the most treacherous enemy of this nation. We must deal with each one of them. The MEK are all criminals. They must all be prosecuted in court. And they must all face the capital punishment. Now is the time to root them out."[125]

These statements and practices demonstrate that Tehran's overall policy vis-à-vis the MEK has undergone a major shift. The regime's behind-the-scenes fear of the MEK has now morphed into an all-out public propaganda campaign fueled with a generous budget. With each passing day, the clerical state's legitimacy is eroded, leading to the irreparable dilution of its conventional cultural and social capacity. The obvious concern of authorities is that the MEK is playing a fundamental role in facilitating the eventual overthrow of the theocracy. That is why Iran is doing everything in its power to neutralize or weaken the MEK or at least to divert or poison public opinion when it comes to the main opposition.

It should also be noted that in 2019, a historical development took place in Albania, where thousands of MEK members reside. Hundreds of politicians and prominent personalities from across the world attended a large international gathering at Ashraf-3, the MEK's new home near the Albanian capital Tirana, for several days.[126] The propaganda spell seemed to be largely broken and the geographical epicenter of resistance against the primary sponsor of terrorism in the world was born and solidified.

The government's multi-faceted soft war against the MEK has been stepped up significantly since then and, judging by the authorities' apparent desperation to blunt the MEK's popularity at home, Tehran's propaganda is unlikely to die down any time soon.

Conclusions and policy recommendations

THE IRANIAN REGIME'S APPROACH TO CONFRONTING the United States and its allies has become increasingly sophisticated and even clever. Today, the regime is nourishing its rogue proxies throughout the Middle East with money and weapons, aiding hostile state and non-state actors in the perpetration of acts of terrorism, violence, and war. The Islamic Republic is also dangerously close to acquiring nuclear weapons capabilities.

Were this insufficient to keep U.S. officials awake at night, recent disclosures suggest that the Iranian regime has infiltrated the U.S. government by placing so-called advisors and specialists in key positions. In so doing, the mullahs have managed to distort American policies and impede U.S. decision-making, with the full extent of the damage yet unknown.

What is clear is that by leveraging mouthpieces, assets, and lobbyists in the United States, the Iranian regime has effectively dictated to U.S. officials what it deems to be *sound policy* toward the Islamic Republic – a policy that views sanctions as unnecessary, anti-government unrest as little more than episodic acts that are to be expected, and the ayatollahs as figures that will fade away unassisted.

Worse still, by allowing Iranian operatives to facilitate a profoundly erroneous, misleading, and disparaging campaign against the ayatollah's formidable pro-democracy foes, the MEK, the U.S. officials have compromised American security interests by leaving policymakers with incorrect and inadequate information to make informed policy choices in both the executive and legislative branches of government.

The primary focus of this book has been to illustrate how Tehran's campaign outside Iran, along with its comprehensive demonization campaign inside the country, constitutes two sides of the same malign effort by the Iranian government to promote itself as a stable and legitimate government while rendering its opposition wholly ineffective.

The fact of the matter is that the MEK is not a tiny sect without support inside the country, nor is it a cult. Preposterous disinformation peddled through insidious influence operations in the West is married with internal propaganda to reinforce the status quo, justify suppression and unthinkable persecution, and ultimately prevent Iranian youth and the public at large from supporting the pro-democracy resistance.

Indeed, falsely characterizing the MEK inside Iran has become a cottage industry that has resulted in the widespread and brutal suppression of the resistance movement's sympathizers and members, with reports of more than 100,000 adherents executed.[127] In 1988 alone, acting on a *fatwa* or religious edict issued by the former supreme leader Khomeini, regime authorities executed some 30,000 political prisoners, mostly MEK activists, in a matter of a few months.[128]

The regime has criminalized even trivially favorable mentions of the MEK through measures that speak to the degree of concern about the group among Iranian officials. According to the Islamic Punishment Act, anyone with ties or links to the MEK is considered an "enemy of God" and must receive the maximum punishment of death.[129]

Nevertheless, the government's forty-plus years of attempts to target the MEK have failed to produce the desired outcome because the MEK's organizational coherence and activism inside the country show no signs of dissipating. Indeed, the state's persistent efforts to counter the organization and its leadership through influence operations and psychological warfare indicate that the MEK and its platform remain as relevant today as it was more than four decades ago.

Today, the new generation in Iran shows a particular curiosity and even attraction to the MEK's staying power. Insofar as the Iranian people deeply mistrust their government, they want to know who the real "hypocrites" – a derogatory label often assigned to the group by Iranian authorities – so despised by the regime are. And they become even more curious when they hear officials, including supreme leader Khamenei, President Raisi, and others, complaining that the MEK is the main organizer of anti-regime sentiment.

Following each wave of protests since 2017, the Iranian regime has become weaker as its base of support has eroded, and economic and social crises have grown more acute. Each uprising has grown, and the people's demands have become more extensive. Ordinary Iranian's readiness to confront the regime's suppressive forces is at an all-time high. Nevertheless, it would be naive to assume that Iran's theocratic rulers will not persist in their policy of repression to the bitter end, refusing to alter their behavior. Consequently, anticipating the ayatollah's collapse from internal factors is a fanciful notion. Every indication points to three conclusions: (1) the overwhelming majority of Iranians want regime change; (2) Tehran's over-reliance on brute force makes the status quo intensely fragile; (3) Iran is ripe for a revolution.

What is also certain is that the Iranian government's denial and deception have failed to eliminate the MEK from Iran's contemporary political landscape. If the past is prologue, the MEK will continue to play a more critical role in Iran's future, including a potential regime change scenario. It would, therefore, be a grave mistake for U.S. officials and Western powers to formulate any policy on Iran without taking the regime's foremost adversary into account.

Appendix

U.S. Senate Letter to Secretary of Defense

United States Senate
WASHINGTON, DC 20510

September 29, 2023

Honorable Lloyd J. Austin II
Secretary of Defense
1000 Defense Pentagon
Washington, DC 20301-1000

Dear Mr. Secretary:

We are concerned that an individual who allegedly served as part of an Iranian Foreign Ministry information operation is currently serving in a senior Department of Defense position. We urge you to take immediate action to ensure that the Department has not been compromised.

On Tuesday, September 26, *Semafor* reported that Ariane Tabatabai, who currently serves as chief of staff to the Assistant Secretary of Defense for Special Operations and Low Intensity Conflict (SOLIC), was part of a so-called Iran Experts Initiative that "senior Iranian Foreign Ministry officials initiated [in] a quiet effort to bolster Tehran's image and positions on global security issues - particularly its nuclear program."

According to communications that *Semafor* reviewed, Ms. Tabatabai agreed to join the Iranian government-linked Initiative in early 2014, after meeting a Germany-based Iranian diplomat in Prague. On at least two occasions, Ms. Tabatabai "checked in with Iran's Foreign Ministry before attending policy events." The report details one occasion in which an Iranian think tank chief, who acted as an apparent liaison to the Iranian Foreign Minister, dissuaded Ms. Tabatabai from participating in a conference in Israel when she asked for his feedback. The report also indicates that Ms. Tabatabai potentially sought the Iranian government's input on a congressional briefing that she was invited to give in July 2014.

Concerns about Ms. Tabatabai are not new. In March 2021, shortly after Ms. Tabatabai was appointed senior adviser in the Office of the Undersecretary of State for Arms Control and International Security, Iranian dissidents noted Ms. Tabatabai's long history of echoing the Iranian regime's talking points. In April 2021, several House members requested a review of Ms. Tabatabai's security clearance. In response, the Biden administration dismissed these allegations as "smears and slander."

The latest allegations reported in *Semafor*, however, indicate that Ms. Tabatabai may have been engaged in a relationship with the Iranian regime well beyond what even her strongest critics alleged. The fact that the Department initially responded to these latest allegations by rushing a full-throated defense of Ms. Tabatabai, rather than taking the time to ensure that our national security has not been compromised, suggests that you are protecting hiring missteps rather than prioritizing national security.

Iran continues to threaten U.S. military personnel in the Middle East and remains intent on assassinating American citizens here in the United States. Given these facts, we find it simply unconscionable that a senior Department official would continue to hold a sensitive position despite her alleged participation in an Iranian government information operation. While we note that Assistant Secretary of Defense for SOLIC Christopher Maier, who is Ms. Tabatabai's current supervisor, testified before the House on Thursday that the Department is "actively looking into whether all law and policy was properly followed in granting my chief of staff top secret special compartmented information," we urge you to suspend Ms. Tabatabai's security clearance immediately pending further review, as the State Department did with her former supervisor, Robert Malley.

In addition, we ask that you provide answers to the following questions no later than October 6:

1. On what date did the Department of Defense learn that Ms. Tabatabai had served as part of the Iranian government-linked Iran Experts Initiative?
2. On what date was Ms. Tabatabai granted a security clearance, and what was the sponsoring agency that made the determination to grant Ms. Tabatabai a security clearance?
3. Has Ms. Tabatabai's security clearance been subjected to a periodic reinvestigation and, if so, on what date was Ms. Tabatabai's most recent periodic reinvestigation completed?
4. Was Ms. Tabatabai subjected to any additional counterintelligence screening, to include a polygraph investigation, as part of her security clearance investigation or any subsequent review of her eligibility to hold a security clearance or access restricted or special access information?
5. On her Standard Form-86, did Ms. Tabatabai list her contacts with:
    a. Former Iranian Foreign Minister Javad Zarif;
    b. Academic Adnan Tabatabai;
    c. Mostafa Zahrani, the head of the Iran think tank IPIS; and/or
    d. Former Iranian Foreign Ministry Spokesman Saeed Khatibzadeh?
6. Was Ms. Tabatabai read into any special access programs (SAPs)?
    a. If so, was she subjected to enhanced security vetting, per SAP security policy, or was she granted a waiver?
    b. If she was granted a waiver to be read into SAPs, which DoD official approved the waiver?

Thank you in advance for your attention to this urgent matter.

Sincerely,

Roger F. Wicker
United States Senator

Charles E. Grassley
United States Senator

Mike Crapo
United States Senator

John Cornyn
United States Senator

Lindsey O. Graham
United States Senator

John Barrasso, M.D.
United States Senator

James E. Risch
United States Senator

Marco Rubio
United States Senator

Ron Johnson
United States Senator

Tim Scott
United States Senator

Ted Cruz
United States Senator

Deb Fischer
United States Senator

Shelley Moore Capito
United States Senator

James Lankford
United States Senator

Tom Cotton
United States Senator

M. Michael Rounds
United States Senator

Thom Tillis
United States Senator

Joni K. Ernst
United States Senator

Dan Sullivan
United States Senator

Todd Young
United States Senator

John Kennedy
United States Senator

Kevin Cramer
United States Senator

Rick Scott
United States Senator

Roger Marshall, M.D.
United States Senator

Bill Hagerty
United States Senator

Tommy Tuberville
United States Senator

Markwayne Mullin
United States Senator

Ted Budd
United States Senator

Eric Schmitt
United States Senator

Katie Boyd Britt
United States Senator

Pete Ricketts
United States Senator

U.S. House of Representatives Letter to Secretary of Defense

COMMITTEE ON ARMED SERVICES
U.S. House of Representatives
Washington, DC 20515-6035
ONE HUNDRED EIGHTEENTH CONGRESS

September 26, 2023

The Honorable Lloyd J. Austin III
Secretary of Defense
1000 Defense Pentagon
Washington, DC 20301

Dear Secretary Austin:

    I write to you to express our deep concern with the Department's hiring of Ariane Tabatabai as the Chief of Staff for Assistant Secretary of Defense for Special Operations and Low Intensity Conflict (ASD/SOLIC). Ms. Tabatabai's past employment history and close ties to the Iranian regime are alarming and should be disqualifying for anyone seeking such a sensitive position of trust within the United States Department of Defense. The Iranian regime is a clear adversary of the United States, and as the world's largest state sponsor of terrorism poses a direct national security threat to United States citizens and interests at home, in the region, and around the globe.

    The Office of ASD SO/LIC oversees many of the Department's most sensitive operations and programs, to include those to counter Iran's malign activities throughout the world. It is the adamant position of the House Committee on Armed Services that no person who aligns themselves with an adversary such as Iran, or who acts as a foreign agent of influence, wittingly or unwittingly, should wield any such influence over United States policy, or have access to such sensitive information.

    We ask for a response to the following questions no later than October 3, 2023:

1. How long has Ms. Tabatabai worked as chief of staff to Assistant Secretary of Defense for Special Operations and Low Intensity Conflict?

2. When did Ms. Tabatabai receive her security clearance?

3. Was she required to go through the Department's Continuous Vetting Process as part of her application process?

September 26, 2023
Secretary Austin
Page 2

4. Are you aware of any instances of Ms. Tabatabai communicating with the Iranian regime, either in her official capacity or unofficially? Are you aware of any communications Ms. Tabatabai had with the Iranian regime prior to her employment?

5. Was the Department aware of Ms. Tabatabai's participation in Iranian government-sponsored influence networks, such as the Iran Experts Initiative?

6. Was Ms. Tabatabai hired as a political appointee, a highly qualified expert, or as a GS employee?

7. What were her unique qualifications with respect to ASD/SOLIC that led to her hiring?

Thank you for your prompt attention to this request. The Committee on Armed Services, under Rule X, clause 1 of the Rules of the House of Representatives (House Rules), maintains oversight jurisdiction over the Department of Defense generally. Moreover, under the House Rules, the Committee on Armed Services derives its authority to conduct oversight from, among other things, clause 2(b)(1) of Rule X (relating to general oversight responsibilities), clause 3(b) of Rule X (relating to special oversight functions), and clause 1(b) of rule XI (relating to investigations and studies).

Sincerely,

Mike Rogers
Chairman
House Committee on Armed Services

Jack Bergman
Chairman
Subcommittee on Intelligence and Special Operations

ABOUT THE AUTHOR
IVAN SASCHA SHEEHAN, PH.D.

Ivan Sascha Sheehan is the associate dean of the College of Public Affairs at the University of Baltimore. He previously served as the executive director of the School of Public and International Affairs between 2018-2023.

A prolific policy-focused scholar, writer, and influential thought leader with a principal focus on terrorism, U.S. foreign policy, international relations, and national security issues, Sheehan joined the University of Baltimore in 2009 after serving on the faculty of the John W. McCormack School of Policy Studies at the University of Massachusetts Boston. A frequent speaker on U.S. foreign policy, Sheehan has addressed diverse audiences from academic forums in Eastern and Western Europe, Asia, the Middle East, and North America to policymakers in the U.S. Congress and the National Press Club. He continues to serve as a subject matter expert and consultant on a range of public policy matters.

Sheehan's early career research focused on quantitative analyses of terrorism incident data and the impact of preemptive force on terrorist activity. In recent years, he has published timely analyses on U.S. policy in the Middle East (Iran, Iraq, Israel, Qatar, Turkey), the Caucasus (Russia, Armenia, Azerbaijan), Asia (North Korea, South Korea, Japan, China), the Balkans (Kosovo, Serbia), Africa (South Africa, Madagascar, Nigeria, Djibouti), and the European Union. Over the course of his career, he has published in peer-reviewed journals on topics related to evidence-based counterterrorism policy, terrorism teaching, terrorist group designations, counterinsurgency, suicide terrorism, and the concept of regime change. He has also undertaken significant research and writing on the Islamic Republic of Iran and U.S. foreign policy in conflict zones across the globe.

The author of almost 200 publications, Sheehan's work has appeared in prominent outlets including *The National Interest, Foreign Policy, Newsweek, U.S. News and World Report, National Review, Fox News, Al Jazeera, The Washington Times, The Hill, Roll Call, The Washington Examiner, The Baltimore Sun, Haaretz* (Israel), *The Jerusalem Post, United Press International,* and *International Policy Digest*. A frequent source for journalists, he has also been quoted in leading newspapers in Ireland and the United Kingdom.

Shared widely around the world, Sheehan's writing has been translated into Farsi, Arabic, French, and Spanish. His work has been cited in testimony in the Canadian parliament, quoted on MSNBC, and endorsed by senior U.S. officials – including a former Director of the FBI, a Secretary of Homeland Security, and an Assistant Secretary of State.

An award-winning scholar, Sheehan received the 2015 President's Faculty Award for outstanding teaching, research, and service and the 2016 University System of Maryland Board of Regents Award for Excellence in Mentoring. These awards are the highest honors bestowed by the University of Baltimore and the University System of Maryland in recognition of exemplary faculty achievements. In 2017, Sheehan received a citation from the Maryland Senate in recognition of "Exceptional leadership and Service to the University of Baltimore."

Prior to assuming leadership of the School of Public and International Affairs, Sheehan was twice elected president of the College of Public Affairs Faculty Senate. He also served as the director of the M.S. in Negotiations and Conflict Management for eight years and was the founding director of the M.A. in Global Affairs and Human Security, a program he led for six years.

Sheehan previously taught at the University of Massachusetts Boston, Bentley University, Tufts University, and George Mason University after earning his Ph.D. in 2006.

IRAN POLICY COMMITTEE (IPC)

The Iran Policy Committee (IPC), established in 2005, is a non-profit, nonpartisan Washington, DC-based research institute focused on US policy toward Iran. For more than fifteen years, IPC has produced actionable research and timely analyses for US officials in the legislative and executive branches, convened briefings on urgent policy matters, made fact-finding trips, interviewed relevant persons, and prompted a closer examination of the prospect of regime change by the Iranian people. IPC's network – which includes former senior White House, State Department, Defense Department, and Intelligence Community officials, as well as prominent scholars from think-tanks and academia – have set forth their recommendations in books, reports, and op-eds, shared their expertise on a bipartisan basis, and participated in interviews and forums around the world. IPC remains committed to educating US officials and the public about the Iranian regime's malign activities and repressive institutions and the pro-democracy opposition seeking an end to clerical rule.

Some of the IPC publications are as follows:

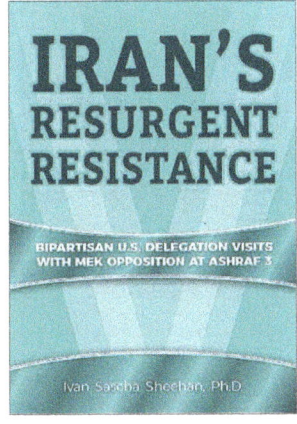
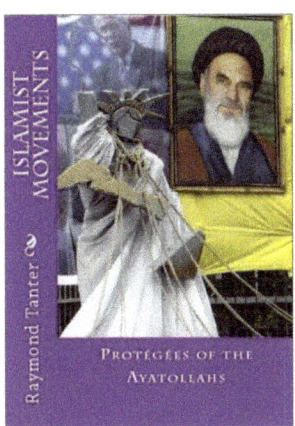

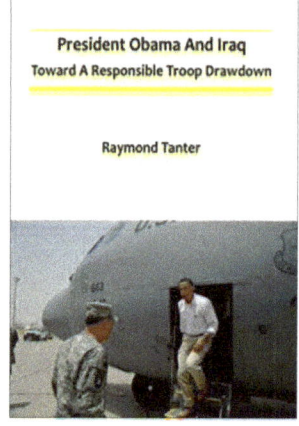

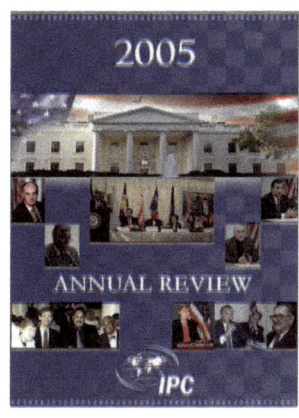

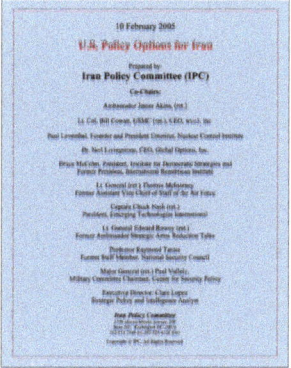
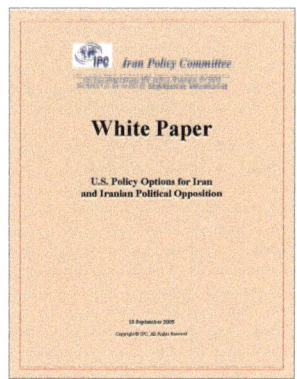

Endnotes

1. Jay Solomon, "Inside Iran's Influence Operations," Last Updated Sep 29, 2023, https://www.semafor.com/article/09/25/2023/inside-irans-influence-operation.

2. Ariane Tabatabai, "Beware of MEK," Last Updated August 22, 2014, https://nationalinterest.org/feature/beware-the-mek-11118.

3. Ariane Tabatabai, *"Terrorism: A Review of the Current Threat Landscape | Panel 3: Iran & Hezbollah,"* Georgetown University, February 5, 2020, Video, 1:12:44, https://youtu.be/vE3F2U4dUPk?t=4363.

4. ibid.

5. Senator Roger Wicker, "Colleagues Demand Accountability on Iran-Linked DoD Official," September 29, 2023, https://www.wicker.senate.gov/2023/9/wicker-colleagues-demand-accountability-on-iran-linked-dod-official.

6. Senators Rick Scott, Ted Cruz and Roger Wicker, "Accountability from Department of Defense after Revelations of Iranian Spy Ring," October 5, 2023, https://www.rickscott.senate.gov/2023/10/sens-rick-scott-ted-cruz-roger-wicker-demand-accountability-from-department-of-defense-after-revelations-of-iranian-spy-ring.

7. Adam Kredo, "GOP Senators Call on Pentagon To Revoke Security Clearance of Official Linked to Iranian Government Group," September 12, 2023, https://freebeacon.com/national-security/gop-senators-call-on-pentagon-to-revoke-security-clearance-of-official-linked-to-iranian-government-group/.

8. Adam Kredo, "Lawmakers Demand State Dept. Revoke Security Clearance for Appointee Tied to Iranian Regime," October 10, 2023, https://freebeacon.com/biden-administration/lawmakers-demand-state-dept-revoke-security-clearance-for-appointee-tied-to-iranian-regime/.

9. Congressmen Mike Rogers and Jack Bergman, "Letter to The Honorable Lloyd J. Austin III Secretary of Defense September 26, 2023, https://armedservices.house.gov/sites/republicans.armedservices.house.gov/files/09.26.23%20Letter%20to%20Secretary%20Austin.pdf.

10. IMF. 2019. "World Economic Outlook, October 2019: Global Manufacturing Downturn, Rising Trade Barriers." The International Monetary Fund. October 2019. https://www.imf.org/en/Publications/WEO/Issues/2019/10/01/world-economic-outlook-october-2019.

11. In April 2020, the Director of the Supreme Audit Court of Iran (SAC), Adel Azar, revealed that a staggering five billion dollars in funds has gone missing. See: "Almost $5 Billion of Iran Government Money for Imports Is Missing." 2020. Radio Free Europe / Radio Liberty. April 15, 2020. https://en.radiofarda.com/a/almost-5-billion-of-iran-government-money-for-imports-is-missing/30554674.html.   Transparency International's 2017 Corruption Perception Index ranks Iran 130 out of 180 countries. See: Transparency International e.V. 2016. "Corruption Perceptions Index 2016." Transparency International. 2016. https://www.transparency.org/news/feature/corruption_perceptions_index_2016.

12. The New York Times wrote in December 2019: "Iran is experiencing its deadliest political unrest since the Islamic Revolution 40 years ago, with at least 180 people killed — and possibly hundreds more — as angry protests have been smothered in a government crackdown of unbridled force." See: Farina Fassihi and Rick Gladstone. 2019. "With Brutal Crackdown, Iran Convulsed by Worst Unrest in 40 Years." *The New York Times*, December 1, 2019. https://www.nytimes.com/2019/12/01/world/middleeast/iran-protests-deaths.html.

13 "The Most Important and Ultimate Ideal Is the Establishment of Islamic Civilization." 2020. Khamenei.ir. May 17, 2020. https://english.khamenei.ir/news/7568/The-most-important-and-ultimate-ideal-is-the-establishment-of.

14 "People's Mojahedin Organization of Iran." 2023. People's Mojahedin Organization of Iran. May 19, 2023. https://english.mojahedin.org/.

15 According to Reuters, the National Council of Resistance of Iran (NCRI) political coalition, which has the MEK as its main component, "has thousands of followers in Europe and the United States and was the first group to expose Iran's overt nuclear program." See: *Reuters*. 2009. "Exiled Iran Opposition Group Holds Big Paris Rally." June 20, 2009, sec. Change Suite. https://www.reuters.com/article/us-iran-election-exiles-sb/exiled-iran-opposition-group-holds-big-paris-rally-idUSTRE55J1BW20090620.

16 Notably, the MEK's social network inside Iran provided the world with the first glimpse of Iran's nuclear weapons program in August 2002. See: The New York Times. 2005. "Chronology of Iran's Nuclear Program." The New York Times. August 8, 2005. https://www.nytimes.com/2005/08/08/international/chronology-of-irans-nuclear-program.html.

17 Shamsi Saadati. 2019. "24th Telethon with Iranian Opposition INTV Satellite Television Network." People's Mojahedin Organization of Iran. December 18, 2019. https://english.mojahedin.org/i/iran-intv-mek-ncri-resistance-units-maryam-rajavi-20191218.

18 Layman, Eric. J. "MEK vows to step up fight against Tehran from new Ashraf-3 base camp." The Washington Times. 2019. "Free Iran Conference Highlights Alleged Iranian Corruption of European Officials." The Washington Times. July 13, 2019. https://www.washingtontimes.com/news/2019/jul/13/free-iran-conference-highlights-alleged-iranian-co/.

19 Providing an in-depth analysis of support for political parties in an environment where freedom of the press and independent polling is severely restricted, is extremely difficult. Still, there are important indicators. For example, in a glimpse of the MEK's following in Iran, on April 19, 2019, Mahmoud Alavi, the Minister of Intelligence said: "Over the past year, 116 teams related to MEK have been dealt with [arrested]." See : "Iran's Intelligence Minister Boasts of Wide-Ranging Successes." 2019. Radio Free Europe / Radio Liberty. April 20, 2019. https://en.radiofarda.com/a/iran-s-intelligence-minister-boasts-of-wide-ranging-successes/29892972.html.   Around the same time, Ministry of Intelligence and Security (MOIS) Director General for East Azerbaijan Province, said: "Last year, the MEK exploited the economic and social problems to expand its activities. Some 60 individuals associated with the group were arrested and 50 more people identified and warned." See: "Vesarat e Ettelaat: Dastgiri e 60 Nafar Az Anazor e Mortabet ba Monafeghin dar Azarbaijan e Sharghi [Intelligence Ministry: Arrest of 60 Person in Connection with the Monafeghin in East-Azerbaijan]." 2019. Asre Iran News Agency. 24 April, 2019. https://www.asriran.com/fa/news/664526/.

20 Sheehan, Ivan Sascha. Iran's Resurgent Resistance: Bipartisan U.S. Delegation Visits with MEK Opposition at Ashraf 3. Iran Policy Committee, 2020.

21 This is supported by many indicators, including statements by officials, including Khamenei (see endnote 22).

22 There have been increasing arrests of people that have joined the MEK's Resistance Units. Mahmoud Alavi, Minister of Intelligence and Security (MOIS), admitted on April 19, 2019, that: "Over the past year, 116 teams associated with the MEK have been dealt with." (State-run Fars News Agency, April 19, 2019). Available at : "Shenasai 290 Jasus dar Mantaghe va Iran/Taghieer E Rahbordi Zedde Jasusi Padafandi Be Afandi [Identification of 290 CIA Spys in the region and Iran/Change in Anti- Espionage Strategy from Defensive to Offensive]". 2019. Fars News Agency. April 19, 2019. https://www.farsnews.ir/news/13980130000225.

23 Several state-run media outlets have published an analysis, which says, among the alternatives to the regime, the regime should focus on the MEK. Did Imam Khomeini not explicitly

say in 1981 that the enemy is not the U.S. or Israel, but the enemy is right here, the MEK? Why do we pointlessly put the name of Reza Pahlavi, who poses no threat to the system, as a distraction along with the name of the real enemy, the MEK, which seeks our downfall. While our supporters continue this wrong method, Massoud Rajavi (leader of the Iranian resistance) constantly speaks of "Resistance Units" and orders chaos and our [regime's] downfall?

24 For example, a Georgetown University study assessed the image of the NCRI/MEK and other Iranian dissident groups, including organizations not espousing regime change. Using the Islamic Republic News Agency (IRNA) for the period from January-December 2005, the study performed a content analysis and "determined the NCRI/MEK was the topic of discussion almost four times as often as all other dissident organizations combined." See: "Preparing for Regime Change in Iran." n.d. The Washington Institute. October 4, 2023. https://www.washingtoninstitute.org/fikraforum/view/preparing-for-regime-change-in-iran.

25 See below section on "Production of movies and TV series defacing the MEK." As recent as the summer of 2020, a well-funded and sensationalist anti-MEK TV series, called the Shahrag (Jugular) was launched in Iran that would be aired in 30 episodes on nation-wide state television. See: "Shahrag, Emshab Rouye Shabake ye Dow [Shahrag, Tonigh on Network 2]." 2020. The Young Reporters Club. June 27, 2020. https://www.yjc.ir/fa/news/7403283/.

26 In July 2019, former justice minister Mostafa Pourmohammadi threatened to exterminate the MEK as a matter of policy. He said: "There has not been a single case of such destruction in the past 40 years, other than those in which the MEK have had the leading role. We have not yet settled the score with the MEK. ... We are going to deal with every single one of them. We will discuss these matters after we eliminate them. We are not joking." (Interview with Mosalas website, July 24, 2019. Transcript (Saadati, Shamsi. 2019. "Top Iran Official Defends 1988 Massacre, Vows to Exterminate the MEK." NCRI. July 30, 2019. https://www.ncr-iran.org/en/news/human-rights/top-iran-official-defends-1988-massacre-vows-to-exterminate-the-mek/.). Watch interview here). Similarly, Ali Razini, a judiciary official, admitted on July 29, 2019 that extrajudicial executions in summer 1988 were carried out on Khomeini's emphatic order "without being held up by red tape." "Iranian Regime Official Admits Extrajudicial Executions of Opponents." 2019. Iran Human rights Monitor. July 30, 2019. https://iran-hrm.com/2019/07/30/iranian-regime-official-admits-extrajudicial-executions-of-opponents/. And, in 1988, according to prominent human rights group Amnesty International, thousands of MEK supporters were killed in what is now known as the "1988 Massacre." See "Iran: Blood-soaked secrets," Amnesty International, December 4, 2018. Available at: "Iran: Blood-Soaked Secrets: Why Iran's 1988 Prison Massacres Are Ongoing Crimes against Humanity." 2018. Amnesty International. December 4, 2018. https://www.amnesty.org/en/documents/mde13/9421/2018/en/.

BBC News. 2021. "France Bomb Plot: Iran Diplomat Assadollah Assadi Sentenced to 20 Years," February 4, 2021, sec. Europe. https://bbc.com/news/world-europe-55931633.

27 See subsequent sections of this report for the number of anti-MEK books, movies, series, and other productions generated by the regime. Moreover, in May 2020, the state-run "Rahyafteha" website revealed the names of some intelligence agents who have been demonizing the MEK for years and who enjoy "a lot of" regime financial backing. "Din e Mobin e Eslam va Karisma ye Shoom e Elteghat [The religion of Islam and the sinister charisma of eclecticism]" Rahyafteha Website. May 29, 2020. https://rahyafteha.ir/85286/.

28 "50 Nafar Az Leaderha ye Eghteshashat e Akhir Monafeghin Boodand [50 Of the Leaders of the Recent Disturbances Where From the Monafeghin]." 2022. IRNA News Agency. November 5, 2022. https://irna.ir/news/84933222/.

29 "Dastgiri ye Afrad e Sazmanyafte dar Eghteshashat [The Arrests of Organized Elements During the Disturbances]." 2022. Mehr News Agency. October 19, 2022. https://mehrnews.com/news/5612765/.

30 State-run Ofogh TV, November 5, 2022.

31 "Iran Judiciary Accuses Detained Students of Terrorist Affiliations." 2020. Radio Free Europe / Radio Liberty. May 5, 2020. https://en.radiofarda.com/a/iran-judiciary-accuses-detained-students-of-terrorist-affiliations/30593802.html.

32 "Iran judiciary admits arresting two elite university students." EU Reporter. May 7, 2020. https://www.eureporter.co/world/iran/2020/05/07/iran-judiciary-admits-arresting-two-elite-university-students/

33 "Iran: Mullahs' Judiciary Admits Arrest of Amir Hossein Moradi and Ali Younesi." NCRI. May 5, 2020. https://www.ncr-iran.org/en/ncri-statements/iran-mullahs-judiciary-admits-arrest-of-amir-hossein-moradi-and-ali-younesi-sharif-university-of-technology-elite-students/.

34 "Biography of Maryam Rajavi." Maryam Rajavi wbsite. n.d. https://www.maryam-rajavi.com/en/biography.

35 For example, former Justice Minister, Mostafa Pourmohammadi said: "Today, the MEK are the most treacherous enemy of this nation." Pourmohammadi's Untold Story of 1988 Events." See: "Nagofte haye Pourmohammadi az Havades e 67 [The Untold Stories of Pourmohammadi of Incidents of 67]." 2019. ISNA News Agency. July 25, 2019. https://isna.ir/news/98050301429/.

36 For example, in May, the regime announced the arrest of two elite students for supporting the MEK, along with 18 others, who were identified by the MEK on May 5. See NCRI website, May 5, 2020. Available at: Iran (NCRI), Secretariat of the National Council of Resistance of. 2020. "Iran: Mullahs' Judiciary Admits Arrest of Amir Hossein Moradi and Ali Younesi, Sharif University of Technology Elite Students." NCRI. May 5, 2020. https://www.ncr-iran.org/en/ncri-statements/iran-mullahs-judiciary-admits-arrest-of-amir-hossein-moradi-and-ali-younesi-sharif-university-of-technology-elite-students/.

37 Mahmoud Alavi, Minister of Intelligence and Security (MOIS), admitted on April 19, 2019, that: "Over the past year, 116 teams associated with the MEK have been dealt with." See: "Shenasaie ye 290 Jassous e CIA dar Mantage va Iran / Tagheere Rahbord e Zedde Jasousi Padafanci be Afandy [Identification of 290 CIA Spys in the region and Iran / Change in Strategy on Anti-Espionoge from Defensive to Offensive]." Fars News Agency. April 19,2019. https://www.farsnews.ir/news/13980130000225/. Since 2017, especially after the relocation of the MEK from Iraq to safety in Albania, the MEK has focused its time and energy on expanding activities of Resistance Units inside Iran. The regime's officials and analysts have become growingly aware of these activities. For example, on December 2, 2018, the state-affiliated website Qaboosnameh said in an analysis: "The recent (2018) protests were the continuation of failed riots of December (2017) led by the MEK. Therefore, this time they have gone to different social sectors. The MEK infiltrates legitimate protest gatherings of the people, using its agents that it calls 'Resistance Units.' Subsequently, a nationwide call is issued by the MEK to expand the gatherings. The 'Resistance Units,' each with a specific number, start their activities." (See: "Vakavie Naghshe Monafeghin dar Harakat e Eterazi Aghshar e Jamee [Disecting the Role of the Monafeghin in the Unrests]." Ghaboosname Website. Accessed October 28, 2023. http://qaboosnameh.ir/news/7563/. Or also see: "Monafeghin, Jabe Siyah e Eghteshashat/Dow Ravayat e Motefavet az Saadabad va Elise [Monafeghin, The Black box of Disturbances/Two Distinct Stories from Saadabad and Elise]." 2023. Qaboos Nameh. October 24, 2023. http://www.qaboosnameh.ir/news/5727/.

38 "Iran's Intelligence Minister Boasts of Wide-Ranging Successes." 2019. Radio Free Europe / Radio Liberty. April 20, 2019. https://en.radiofarda.com/a/iran-s-intelligence-minister-boasts-of-wide-ranging-successes/29892972.html.

39 admin-hr. 2019. "Four Prisoners of the Evin Prison Were Sentenced to Death and Imprisonment." Hrana. May 22, 2019. https://www.en-hrana.org/four-prisoners-of-the-evin-prison-were-sentenced-to-death-and-imprisonment.

40 In October 2019, Albania revealed the names of an alleged Iranian terrorist cell that was plotting to attack the MEK base in Albania. See: "Albania Names Iranian, Turkish Members of Alleged Terrorist Cell." 2019. Voice of America. October 23, 2019. https://www.voanews.com/europe/albania-names-iranian-turkish-members-alleged-terrorist-cell. In July 2018, Iranian intelligence operatives were charged with trying to bomb a massive MEK rally near Paris. See: "Couple Is Charged in Plot to Bomb Iranian Opposition Rally in France." The New York Times, July 2, 2018. https://www.nytimes.com/2018/07/02/world/europe/iran-france-belgium-bomb.html.

41 In January 2020, in a televised speech, Iran's supreme leader Khamenei lamented the "small and sinister" country of Albania for hosting thousands of "treacherous" MEK members. Khamenei added that the MEK "drew up plans" to lead the nationwide protests in November 2019. Albanian leaders hit back. See "Albanian Leaders Dismiss Khamenei's Purported 'Sinister' Smear." Radio Free Europe Radio Liberty, January 9, 2020. https://www.rferl.org/a/albanian-leaders-dismiss-khamenei-s-purported-sinister-smear/30368335.html. In a speech, days after December 2017 major protests broke out, Khamenei, acknowledged the MEK's leading role and said based on evidence and intelligence: "The MEK had prepared for this [protest] months ago. ... The MEK's media outlet had called for it." Khamenei's website, January 9, 2018. http://english.khamenei.ir/news/5394/Recent-damage-inflicted-on-Iran-by-U-S-will-gain-a-response. At the same time, Iranian president Hassan Rouhani complained about the MEK's presence in France in a phone call with his French counterpart Emmanuel Macron, and "asked Macron to take action against a Paris-based Iranian opposition group called the Mujahedeen-e-Khalq, who he accused of fomenting the recent protests." See "Macron 'Worried About Iran, Asks Rouhani for 'Restraint.'" *Agence France Presse*, January 3, 2018. https://en.radiofarda.com/a/iran-protests-macron-rouhani/28951795.html.

42 Reza Hosseini, the advisor of the headquarters of Armed Forces Cyber Warfare. *Fars News Agency* (affiliated to the IRGC), August 1, 2018.

43 In addition, the tools outlined in the footnote below, the regime spends large sums of money abroad to discredit the MEK. For example, the Canadian newspaper Toronto Sun has revealed that John Thompson, who heads up the Mackenzie Institute think tank, "was offered $80,000 by a man tied to Iran's mission in Canada. He said: "They wanted me to publish a piece on the Mujahedin-e khalq. ... Iran is trying to get other countries to label it as a terrorist cult." Thompson says he turned down the offer." (Toronto Sun, July 5, 2020. Available at: "Activists Say Spy Chief Is Right, China Is Spying | Canada | News | Toronto Sun." 2010. Web. archive.org. July 8, 2010. http://web.archive.org/web/20100708150317/https://torontosun.com/news/canada/2010/07/05/14616126.html.

44 In this regard, in May 2020, the state-run "Rahyafteha" website revealed the names of some of the regime's intelligence agents who have been demonizing the MEK for years and who enjoy "a lot of [Intelligence Ministry] energy and of course financial backing." The article says in part: "The office of [Mahmoud] Alavi, the honorable minister of security and intelligence, is working around the clock and has hired some of the MEK's repentant defectors such as Soltani, Khodabandeh, Ezati, Hosseini, Karimdadi, Mesdaghi, Yaghmai, Pour-Hossain, and… By putting a lot of energy and of course, financially backing them, it uses them to psychologically confront the MEK, which is great, but is it enough?" See: "Din e Mobin e Eslam va Karismaye Shoom e Elteghat [The religion of Islam and the sinister charisma of eclecticism]." Rahyafteha website. May 29, 2020. https://rahyafteha.ir/85286/.

45 An IRGC official said its domestic arm has "21,000" honorary "reporters." They work with the IRGC, he added, in "cultural fields." Ramezan Sharif said: "Since the IRGC and the Bassij have various media outlets across the country, throughout every year they set up required training sessions for reporters. See "Sazmandehi ye 21hezar Khabarnegar e Eftekhari dar Basij [21,000 honorary reporters organized in Bassij.]" Fars news agency, October 7, 2011. https://web.archive.org/web/20180501160508/http://www.farsnews.com/newstext.php?nn=13900715000326.

Additionally, the mission of the paramilitary Basij, tied to the Islamic Revolutionary Guard Corps (IRGC), "can be broadly defined as ... enforcing ideological and Islamic values and combating the 'Western cultural onslaught.' See: "Pillar of the State." n.d. RadioFreeEurope/RadioLiberty. https://www.rferl.org/a/Irans_Basij_Force_Mainstay_Of_Domestic_Security/1357081.html.

46 Wilford, John Noble. 1972. "1943 O.S.S. Study Called Hitler Weak and a Bully." *The New York Times*, September 10, 1972, sec. Archives. https://www.nytimes.com/1972/09/10/archives/1943-oss-study-called-hitler-weak-and-a-bully-1943-psychoanalytic.html.

47 Ibid.

48 Langer, Walter C. "A Psychological Analysis of Adolph Hitler: His Life and Legend." Central Intelligence Agency, Release date July 28, 1998. p. 51. See: "Freedom of Information Act Electronic Reading Room | CIA FOIA (Foia.cia.gov)." n.d. Www.cia.gov. Accessed October 29, 2023. https://www.cia.gov/library/readingroom/document/cia-rdp78-02646r000600240001-5.

49 Hitler, Adolf. *Mein Kampf*. Houghton Mifflin, 1999.

50 According to the U.S. State Department, "Iran is the world's leading state sponsor of terrorism. Period. It has held that dubious distinction for many years now and shows no sign of relinquishing the title." See Sales, Nathan. "Countering Iran's Global Terrorism." *U.S. Department of State*, November 13, 2018. https://www.state.gov/countering-irans-global-terrorism/.

51 The regime's former justice minister said in 2019 that the MEK "destroy your image all around the world. There has not been a single case of such destruction in the past 40 years, other than those in which the MEK have had the leading role." (Interview with Mosalas website, July 24, 2019. Transcript here: Saadati, Shamsi. 2019. "Top Iran Official Defends 1988 Massacre, Vows to Exterminate the MEK." NCRI. July 30, 2019. https://www.ncr-iran.org/en/news/human-rights/top-iran-official-defends-1988-massacre-vows-to-exterminate-the-mek/. Watch interview here: "Service e Eshterak e Video [Aparat Subscription Service]." Aparat Video. Accessed October 29, 2023. https://www.aparat.com/v/EY749/.

52 Mohammad-Reza Marandi, interview with state-run *Jam-e Jam* TV, August 30, 2019. Available at: "Tahrif e Tarikh ya Jang e Ravani [Fabrication of Historical facts or a Phsycological War?] State-run Jam-e Jam TV. August 30, 2019. https://vimeo.com/360980369.

53 "The MEK leader Massoud Rajavi at the time campaigned for President saying he would improve on Khomeini's constitution which was based on *Velayat-e faqih* (guardianship of the Islamic jurist) and amounted to dictatorship. Writing in 1981, George W. Ball, who had been Under Secretary of State and then US Ambassador to the UN under Presidents Kennedy and Johnson, commented that the MEK's "intention is to replace the current backward Islamic regime with a modernized Shiite Islam drawing its egalitarian principles from Koranic sources rather than Marx." See: Bloomfield, Lincoln P. Jr. *The Mujahedin-e Khalq MEK: Shackled by a Twisted History*. University of Baltimore, 2013. P. 23. https://www.amazon.com/Mujahedin-Khalq-Shackled-Twisted-History/dp/0615783848

54 Abrahamian, Ervand. *Radical Islam: The Iranian Mojahedin*. Tauris, 1989. P. 213.

55 At one point, starting in 1984, the MEK and NCRI peace proposal "received widespread international support. More than 6,000 members of parliaments and distinguished political and social figures, together with more than 220 political parties, organizations, associations, and trade unions from fifty-seven countries around the world, signed an international declaration which supported the NCRI peace plan." See Mohaddessin, Mohammad. *Enemies of the Ayatollahs: The Iranian Opposition's War on Islamic Fundamentalism*. Zed Books, 2004. P. 112.

56 "Iran: Blood-Soaked Secrets: Why Iran's 1988 Prison Massacres Are Ongoing Crimes Against Humanity." *Amnesty International*, December 4, 2018. https://www.amnesty.org/en/documents/mde13/9421/2018/en/.

57   On May 9, 2003, at a press briefing, the U.S. Department of State spokesman, Richard Boucher, said: "Iran has acknowledged both the heavy water production plant at Arak and the uranium enrichment facility at Natanz, but did so only after their existence was disclosed to the press in August 2002 by an Iranian opposition group." See "Iranian Nuclear Facilities: Arak and Natanz (Taken Question)." U.S. Department of State, May 9, 2003. https://2001-2009.state.gov/r/pa/prs/ps/2003/20439.htm.

58   See, for example, "Amnesty International Outraged at Execution of a 16-Year-Old Girl." *Amnesty International*, April 12, 2016. <https://www.scoop.co.nz/stories/WO0408/S00230/iran-reported-execution-of-a-16-year-old-girl.htm>

59   In January 2020, in a televised speech, Iran's supreme leader Khamenei lamented the "small and sinister" country of Albania for hosting thousands of "treacherous" MEK members. Khamenei added that the MEK "drew up plans" to lead the nationwide protests in November 2019. Albanian leaders hit back. See "Albanian Leaders Dismiss Khamenei's Purported 'Sinister' Smear." Radio Free Europe Radio Liberty, January 9, 2020. https://www.rferl.org/a/albanian-leaders-dismiss-khamenei-s-purported-sinister-smear/30368335.html. In a speech, days after December 2017 major protests broke out, Khamenei acknowledged the MEK's leading role and said based on evidence and intelligence: "The MEK had prepared for this [protest] months ago. … The MEK's media outlet had called for it." Khamenei's website, January 9, 2018. http://english.khamenei.ir/news/5394/Recent-damage-inflicted-on-Iran-by-U-S-will-gain-a-response.   At the same time, Iranian president Hassan Rouhani complained about the MEK's presence in France in a phone call with his French counterpart Emmanuel Macron, and "asked Macron to take action against a Paris-based Iranian opposition group called the Mujahedeen-e-Khalq, who he accused of fomenting the recent protests." See "Macron 'Worried About Iran, Asks Rouhani for 'Restraint'." *Agence France Presse*, January 3, 2018. https://en.radiofarda.com/a/iran-protests-macron-rouhani/28951795.html.

60   For example, the Canadian newspaper Toronto Sun has revealed that John Thompson, who heads the Mackenzie Institute think tank, "was offered $80,000 by a man tied to Iran's mission in Canada. He said: "They wanted me to publish a piece on the Mujahedin-e khalq. … Iran is trying to get other countries to label it as a terrorist cult." Thompson says he turned down the offer." See: "Activists Say Spy Chief Is Right, China Is Spying | Canada | News | Toronto Sun." 2010. Web.archive.org. July 8, 2010. http://web.archive.org/web/20100708150317/https://torontosun.com/news/canada/2010/07/05/14616126.html.

61   As just one example, in May 2020, the state-run "Rahyafteha" website revealed the names of some of the regime's intelligence agents who have been recruited to carry out propaganda against the MEK. The article says in part: "The office of [Mahmoud] Alavi, the honorable minister of security and intelligence, is working around the clock and has hired some of the MEK's repentant defectors such as Soltani, Khodabandeh, Ezati, Hosseini, Karimdadi, Mesdaghi, Yaghmai, Pour-Hossain, and… By putting a lot of energy and of course, financially backing them, it uses them to psychologically confront the MEK, which is great, but is it enough?" (Rahyafteha website, May 29, 2020. https://rahyafteha.ir/85286/.)

62   "Special Report: Iran's leader ordered crackdown on unrest - 'Do whatever it takes to end it.'" *Reuters*, December 23, 2019. https://www.reuters.com/article/us-iran-protests-specialreport/special-report-irans-leader-ordered-crackdown-on-unrest-do-whatever-it-takes-to-end-it-idUSKBN1YR0QR.

63   See above footnotes (17 and 28).

64   On the anniversary of the 2009 anti-regime protests in Iran in 2015, several state-run media outlets in Iran intensified a wave of attacks against the MEK for their role in the protests. The main state-run TV channel aired a speech that Maryam Rajavi, the NCRI's president-elect, delivered before the protest began. In her speech she revealed the mullahs' plans to rig the elections. The TV channel concluded that the MEK has had an extensive role in the protests. See "Iranian government affiliate media attack opposition," PMOI, February 1, 2015.

65   The regime has tried to issue death sentences to intimidate the population and prevent further uprisings. In June 2020, the head of judiciary in Isfahan said: "Puppet of the MEK should know that if a violation were to occur like those that occurred in 2009, 2017 and November of last year, we will certainly and firmly confront puppets and rioters. Today, 8 cases relating to the mentioned occurrences were finalized and charges of corruption on earth [carrying the death penalty] were proven." See: "Hokm e Mofsed e Fee Alarz baraye Parvande ye Eterazat Day 96 va Aban e 98 [Corruption on Earth charges for 8 cases in December 2017 and November 2019 cases]." state-run Hamshahri daily, June 27, 2020. https://www.hamshahrionline.ir/news/525920/.

66   See recent examples at "The trail of blood on TV," state-run Jam-e Jam, July 18, 2020. https://www.magiran.com/article/4065924/ . Other productions are mentioned by the regime's media outlets. For example, see "Films produced about the MEK," state-run Mashreq News daily, September 28, 2016. https://www. mashreghnews.ir/news/636809/. "The MEK in cinema and on TV," State-run Tasnim news agency, June 11, 2017. https://www.tasnimnews.com/fa/news/1396/03/21/1433141/. "Film hayee ke darbareh ye Monafeghin Sakhte Shode ast [Movies Produced Regarding the Monafeghin]." 2016. Mashregh News. September 28, 2016. https://mashreghnews.ir/news/636809/.

67   "Shahedan e Eini az Nagofte haye engelab Khabar Midahand Dar Sarcheshmeh Sarihim [Eye Witnesses Tell of the Untold Stories of the Revolution / We are explicit in Sarcheshmeh]." Quds Online. December 25, 2019. http://qudsonline.ir/news/684699/.

68   "Bazar e Daghe Film haye Amniyati va Zaeghe ye Siyasypasand e Davaran [The Hot Market of Security Films and The Pro-political Taste of Judges]." 2023. Hamshahri Online. October 24 2023. https://hamshahrionline.ir/news/484917/.

69   "Taghdear e Rahbari az Ghallade haye Tala: Afarin, Afarin, Afarin [Leader's Appreciation for the Golden Collars: Well Done, Well Done, Well Done]." 2018. Asre Iran. December 30, 2018. https://asriran.com/fa/news/647226/.

70   "Bazar e Daghe Film haye Amniyati va Zaeghe ye Siyasypasand e Davaran [The Hot Market of Security Films and The Pro-political Taste of Judges]." 2023. Hamshahri Online. October 24 2023. https://hamshahrionline.ir/news/484917/.

71   Ibid.

72   "Warrior, interrogator, artist," Radio Farda, August 11, 2020. https://en.radiofarda.com/a/warrior-interrogator-artist-the-man-who-leads-irgc-s-cultural-onslaught/30778529.html.

73   For example: "IRGC-affiliated news agencies basically consider the launch of "Owj" as a response of Mohammad Hassani and his associates to the "call of Ain-a Ammar" of the Supreme Leader of the Islamic Republic after the events of 2009 to "revive" the "Cultural Front of the Revolution." For example see: "Raees e Sazman e Owj; Bazjoo, Rafigh e Haj Ghasem va Modafe Haram [The interrogator, friend of Haj Qasim and defender of the shrine]." Radio Farda. August 11, 2020. https://www.radiofarda.com/a/who-leading-owj-which-dominating-Iranian-cinema/30777906.html.

74   According to the Journal, "The IRGC Intelligence Organization is now headed by Hojjatoleslam Hossein Taeb with Hojjatoleslam Gholamhossein Ramezani as his counterintelligence chief.22 Taeb's organization is headquartered at Qasr-e Firouzeh in Kamali near Tehran. Taeb's IRGC Intelligence Organization also commands the Internal Security Directorate at MOIS and the security apparatus of the Basiji." See: Wege, Carl. n.d. "Guide to the Study of Intelligence Iran's Intelligence Establishment." AFIO. Summer 2015. https://www.afio.com/publications/WEGE%20Iranian%20Intel%20Services%202015%20 Sep%2001%20FINAL.pdf.

75   "Gozaresh|Ba Savabegh e Janeshin va Moaaven e Hamahang Konandeh ye Jadid e Sepah Ashna Shavid [Report|Become Familiar with Background Profile of the New Deputy and

Coordinator of the IRGC]." 2019. Tasnim News Agency. May 16, 2019. https://tasnimnews.com/fa/news/1398/02/26/2012971/.

76 "The next Battlefield for Iran's Generals Is the Movies." 2021. Newlines Magazine. July 6, 2021. https://newlinesmag.com/essays/iran-takes-its-global-wars-to-the-movies/.

77 With respect to the latest uprisings in November 2019, for example, The New York Times reported: "Most of the nationwide unrest seemed concentrated in neighborhoods and cities populated by low-income and working-class families, suggesting this was an uprising born in the historically loyal power base of Iran's post-revolutionary hierarchy." See Farnaz Fassihi, and Rick Gladstone. "With Brutal Crackdown, Iran Is Convulsed by Worst Unrest in 40 Years." The New York Times, December 1, 2019. https://www.nytimes.com/2019/12/01/world/middleeast/iran-protests-deaths.html.

78 "Pardeh Bardarye Mahmoud Alavi az Name Tolidate Cinamaiee va Televisionye Vezarate Ettelaat [Mahmoud Alavi unveiled the name of the Ministry of Information's film and television productions]."Radio Farda Website (Farsi). February 9, 2021. https://www.radiofarda.com/a/31094421.html.

79 "Eftekhare Ma Ein Ast ke az Hich Sefaratkhaneye Khareji Pool Nemigirim [We are proud to not receive any money from any foreign embassy]." (In Farsi). State-run ISNA News Agency, August 7, 2017. https://www.isna.ir/news/96051609790/.

80 "Sepah Niyazi be Shabakeh ye Mostaghelleh Televisioni Nadarad/Tolidat e 'Oaj' Mahsoul e Sepah Nist [IRGC Has no Need for a Separate TV Network/ 'Oaj' Productions are not Work of IRGC]."2014. Mehr News Agency. December 10, 2014. https://mehrnews.com/news/2418602/.

81 "Owj soon became the leading player in Iran's cinema, theater, music, graphic art, and urban graphics." Radio Farda, August 11, 2020. "Warrior, Interrogator, Artist; the Man Who Leads IRGC's Cultural Onslaught." n.d. RFE/RL. https://en.radiofarda.com/a/warrior-interrogator-artist-the-man-who-leads-irgc-s-cultural-onslaught/30778529.html.

82 "Dr. Raz Zimmt Main Argument." 2018. https://www.terrorism-info.org.il/app/uploads/2018/07/E_170_18.pdf.

83 "According to the news, this film [Cyanide] was produced under the direct supervision of the Ministry of Intelligence and its story is about [the Mojahedin]" (Tasnim - October 8, 2016). https://tinyurl.com/nf6pavzs. "Siyanoor; Filmi ke Havashiye on Payani Nadarad ["Cyanide"; A movie that has no end]." Tasnim News Agency. October 8, 2016. https://www.tasnimnews.com/fa/news/1395/07/17/1207521/.

84 "Dolatha Farhang ra baraye Vitrin e Entekhabat Mikhahand / 8 Miliyard Boodjeh e Film e Jadid e <Hatamikia> / Mozakereh ba <Sami Yousef> baraye Bargozarie Concert dar Iran [Government Wants Culture to be the Showcase for the Elections / 8 Billion Was the Budjet for 'Hatami Kia' New Movie / Negociations with 'Sami Yusef' for Holding a Concert in Iran]." 2017. Fars News Agency. August 7, 2017. https://www.farsnews.ir/news/13960516000578/.

85 On its website, Khaneh Tarrahan describes one of its missions as "promoting and safeguarding values of the Islamic Revolution and the Sacred Defense (meaning the Iran-Iraq War). See: http://khanetarrahan.ir/

86 https://www.entekhab.ir/fa/news/642905/

87 "'Bazy e Taj-o-Takht e 2' Ba Hozoor e Hatamikia ['Game of Thrones 2' with Hatami Kia]." 2010. Khabar Online. February 14, 2010. http://khabaronline.ir/news/754599/.

88 "Iran's Intelligence Ministry Makes Movies in Europe, Trumpets Islamic Republic's Narrative." 2020. Radio Free Europe / Radio Liberty. February 21, 2020. https://en.radiofarda.com/a/iran-s-intelligence-ministry-makes-movies-in-europe-trumpets-islamic-republic-s-narrative/30446893.html.

89   "Journal of Iran's Cinema." 2023. Cinema Journal. October 24, 2023. https://www.cinema-journal.ir/.

90   "Fajr Film Festival Announces Nominations." 2016. Mehr News Agency. February 10, 2016. https://en.mehrnews.com/news/114334/Fajr-Film-Festival-announces-nominations.

91   "Morteza Esfahani Rouzgari Ozve Vezarate Ettelaat Jomhourie Eslami Boudeh ["Morteza Esfahani Was Once an Islamic Republic Intelligence Agent.]." Iran Wire, May 22, 2018. https://www.iranwire.com/fa/blogs/26193/.

92   "Mard e Posht e Sahne ye 'Majeray e Nimrooz' va 'Shabi ke Mah Kamel Shod' Keist? [Who is the Man Behind the Scenes of 'Mid-day Incident' and 'The Night that the Moon Was Complete?']." 2019. Tabnak News. July 4, 2019. https://tabnak.ir/fa/news/909515/. Also see: "Majera ye Ashnaie ye Behrooz Afkhami ba Maamour e Ettelaat [The Story Behind the Acquaintance of Behrooz Afkhami and the Intelligence Agent?]." 2015. Mehr News Agency. February 6, 2015. https://mehrnews.com/news//2488656.

93   "Iran's Intelligence Ministry Makes Movies in Europe, Trumpets Islamic Republic's Narrative." Radio Farda, February 21, 2020. https://en.radiofarda.com/a/iran-s-intelligence-ministry-makes-movies-in-europe-trumpets-islamic-s-narrative/30446893.html.

94   "Majaray-e Nimrouz Continues." Sobh-e No, July 17, 2017. https://sobhe-no.ir/newspaper/274/11/10479.

95   "Mard e Posht e Sahne ye 'Majeray e Nimrooz' va 'Shabi ke Mah Kamel Shod' Keist? [Who is the Man Behind the Scenes of 'Mid-day Incident' and 'The Night that the Moon Was Complete?']."2019. Tabnak News. July 4, 2019. https://tabnak.ir/fa/news/909515/.

96   "Iran: Alarming Pattern of Killings and 'Disappearances.'" 1998. Amnesty International. https://www.amnesty.org/en/wp-content/uploads/2021/06/mde130251998en.pdf.

97   Archives, L. A. Times. 1999. "Suspect in Iran Slayings Kills Self, Official Says." Los Angeles Times. June 21, 1999. https://www.latimes.com/archives/la-xpm-1999-jun-21-mn-48725-story.html.

98   "Chetor Vezarate Ettelaat da Ghalbe Orupa Film Sakht? [How did the Inteligance Ministry Produced a Movie at the Heart of Europe?]." Radio Farda. February 20, 2020. https://www.radiofarda.com/a/Unveiling-of-security-agent-who-appears-as-screenwriter-in-Iranian-movies/30443184.html.

99   Ibid.

100 "Farhad Tohidi; Morteza Esfahani Az Tarafe Kargardan be Onvane Mottalee be Man Moarefi Shod [Farhad Tohidi, Moteza Esfahani Was Introduced to me as a Knowledgeable Person]." Iran Wire. May 22, 2018. https://iranwire.com/fa/blogs/838/26160.

101 "1988: The Crime That won't Go Away." Iran Wire. August 3, 2017. https://iranwire.com/en/features/4745.

102 "Hame ye Ajzaye Film e Nimrooz Aali Bood / Khatereh ye Montasher Nashode Rahbar e Moaazam e Enghelab e Eslami as Rooz e Paksazi Khaneh Mousa Khiyabani [All Parts of the Movie 'Mid-day Incedent' was Fine / An Unpublished Memory of the Highness the Leader of the Islamic Revolution about the day of Clearance at Mousa Khiyabani's House]." 2017. Mizan Online. July 15, 2017. https://mizanonline.com/fa/news/328873.

103 "Owj Arts and Media Organization." 2023. Wikipedia. June 28, 2023. https://en.wikipedia.org/wiki/Owj_Arts_and_Media_Organization.

104 "TV Network of Islamic Republic." 2014. Wikipedia.org. Wikimedia Foundation, Inc. June 3, 2014. https://fa.wikipedia.org/wiki/%D8%B4%D8%A8%DA%A9%D9%87_%D8%A7%D9%81%D9%82.

105 "Shabakeh ye Ofogh Rasman Aghaz be Kar Kard / Tavajoh e Vijeh be Mousique ['Ofogh' Network Officially Started Operation / Special Attention to Music]." 2015. Mehr News Agency. February 27, 2015. https://mehrnews.com/news/2507756/.

106 "Hamayesh e Meli 'Naghshe Daneshgah-ha va Hozeh-ha dar Tahavolle Hendesseh ye Ghodrat e Jahani[The Strategic Role of Universities and Religious Schools in the Transformation of Geometry of Power in Global Scale]." 2012. Tasnim News. December 15, 2012. https://tasnimnews.com/fa/news/1391/09/25/4961/.

107 Ibid.

108 "IRIB Ofogh." 2023. Wikipedia. September 29, 2023. https://en.wikipedia.org/wiki/IRIB_Ofogh.

109 "Shabakey ye Televisioni ye Ofogh ba Naghshafarini ye Hamiyan e Ahmadinejad va Jebhe ye Paydari rouye Anten e Seda va Sima [Ofogh Television Network with Active Participation of Ahmadinejad Supporters and Stability Front Broadcasting on the National TV Seda-va-Sima]."2014. Khabar Online. June 23, 2014. https://khabaronline.ir/news/361700/.

110 "Paygahe Jame e Ettela Resani ye Sima [Sima News Website]." IRIB TV. Accessed October 30, 2023. http://www.iribtv.ir/portal/newsview/17361.

111 "Aparat Television Video Subscriptions" Aparat TV. October 30,2023. https://www.aparat.com/result/%D8%AC%D9%87%D8%A7%D9%86_%D8%A2%D8%B1%D8%A7.

112 "Sokout e Diplomacy ye Farhangi dar Moghabel e Harzegouiee ye Monafeghin [Silence of Cultural Diplomacy Against Obscenity of Hypocrates]."2018. Mashregh News. July 3, 2018. https://mashreghnews.ir/news/744569/.

113 "Monafeghin dar Cinema, from 'Tavahom' to 'Radde Khoon' [Monafeghin in the Movies, from 'Illusion' to "Trails of Blood']." 2019. Javan Online. August 6, 2019. https://javanonline.ir/fa/news/964884/.

114 "Bastareh Asli ye Faaliat Monafeghin Resane Ast [The Main Area of Activities of the Monafeghin is the Media]." 2019. Javan Online. January 31, 2019. https://javanonline.ir/fa/news/944310/.

115 "Goodarzi: Talash Kardim Dast e Monafeghin ra baraye Mardom Roo Konim ta Digar Jaye Jallad va Shahid Avaz Nashavad [Goodarzi: We tried to expose the Monafeghin Actions so No Longer Would the place of Killers and Martyrs be Switched]." 2018. Javan Online. December 24, 2018. https://javanonline.ir/fa/news/939287/.

116 "Blood-Soaked Secrets." 2018. Amnesty International. October 31, 2018. https://amnesty.org/en/latest/campaigns/2018/10/blood-soaked-secrets/.

117 Writer, Staff. 2016. "Statements of Support on Relocation of PMOI (MEK) from Camp Liberty in Iraq." NCRI. September 18, 2016. https://ncr-iran.org/en/news/iran-resistance/statements-of-support-on-relocation-of-pmoi-mek-from-camp-liberty-in-iraq/.

118 "Iran Still Seeks to Erase the '1988 Prison Massacre' from Memories, 25 Years On." 2013. Amnesty International. August 29, 2013. https://amnesty.org/en/latest/news/2013/08/iran-still-seeks-erase-prison-massacre-memories-years/.

119 "Tehran: Bish as 300 Namayeshgah ba Mozoo e Monafeghin dar Keshvar Barpa Shodeh Ast [Tehran: Over 300 Exhibitions Have Been Held in the Country on the topic of Monafeghin]." Halghe Vasl. February 11, 2017. http://hvasl.ir/news/23803.

120 "Namayeshgah e Aks e Amaliat e Mersad Barpa Mishavad [Picture Exhibition of the Mersad Operation Will be Held]." 2023. Fars News Agency. October 25 2023. http://fashnews.ir/fa/news-details/68342/.

121 "Namayeshgahe Amaliate Mersad [Mersad Operation Exhibition]." Habilian Website. Accessed October 30, 2023. https://www.habilian.ir/fa/main/category-5/category-101.html.

122 "Sardar Jalali: Moghabele ba Nefagh dar Faza ye Majazi as 'Mersad' Sakht tar Ast [Jalali: Confronting the Monafeghin on the Internet is Harder than 'Mersad' Operation]." 2019. ISNA New Agency. July 29, 2019. https://isna.ir/news/98050703424/.

123 "Service e Eshterak e Video ye Aparat [Aparat Video Subscription Service]." N.D. Aparat. Accessed October 25, 2023. https://aparat.com/v/4NH3Q/.

124 "Iran: Key Officials Named over 1988 Mass Prison Killings - New Report." n.d. Www.amnesty.org.uk. Accessed October 25, 2023. https://www.amnesty.org.uk/press-releases/iran-key-officials-named-over-1988-mass-prison-killings-new-report/.

125 "Nagofte haye Pourmohammadi az Havades e 67 [The Untold Stories of Pourmohammadi of Incidents of 67]." 2019. ISNA News Agency. July 25, 2019. https://isna.ir/news/98050301429/.

126 www.washingtontimes.com, The Washington Times https. n.d. "Special Section: Iran: The Power of the Alternative." The Washington Times. Accessed October 25, 2023. https://www.washingtontimes.com/specials/free-iran-rally-2019-washington-dc/.

127 Bloomfield, Lincoln, Ivan Foreword, and Sheehan. n.d. "The Ayatollahs and the MEK Iran's Crumbling Influence Operation." Accessed October 25, 2023. http://www.ubalt.edu/about-ub/news-events/images/The%20Ayatollahs%20and%20the%20MEK.pdf.

128 Writer, Staff. 2008. "A Shocking Confession by a Former Top MOIS Official." NCRI. October 23, 2008. https://www.ncr-iran.org/en/news/iran-resistance/a-shocking-confession-by-a-former-top-mois-official/.

129 United Nations High Commissioner for Refugees. 2019. "Refworld | Iran: Islamic Penal Code." Refworld. 2019. https://www.refworld.org/docid/518a19404.html.

www.ingramcontent.com/pod-product-compliance
Lightning Source LLC
Chambersburg PA
CBHW061740070526
44585CB00024B/2750